"Having just returned from two weeks in Turke[__] [__] of the seven churches mentioned in the boo[__] how the early disciples acted with such courage, creativity, and cultural awareness to turn their world upside down. Ever since, I've been wondering how we got so far away from that early sense of mission and how we can recapture that in our twenty-first-century world?

In his refreshing book *Parallel Faith*, Dave Boden provides us with a wonderfully engaging call to disciple-making for today's culture. It's an inspiring, practical, and winsome exploration of Jesus' command to make disciples. Boden explores how we can recapture the heart of disciple-making without using gimmicks or pressure for conversions, but in being true friends in close proximity in the ordinariness of others' lives.

Dave emphasizes a process of walking alongside others aiming for transformation in Jesus and not settling for a simple transaction with a stale, one-size-fits-all message. Filled with thoughtful reflection questions, insightful illustrations, and engaging stories, *Parallel Faith* helps ordinary disciples take courageous steps to listen generously to others, reframe the misconceptions of Jesus held by many, and creatively demonstrate the hope that is in Jesus Christ. Readers will benefit tremendously from Dave's abundant experience and the wonderfully rich practical applications. I can hardly wait to give it out to my friends, colleagues, and those I train to take the good news of Christ to a seemingly foreign culture in our day!"

**—Brett Andrews, director of People Development,
Youth for Christ Canada**

"Companionship has too often been lost to consumption in our modern approach to Christianity. But relationships will always be the wineskin of the Word incarnate. *Parallel Faith* is a much-needed manifesto to help restore the heart of Jesus for walking alongside others."

**—Ben Arment, author of *Dream Year:
Make the Leap from a Job You Hate to a Life You Love***

"Dave is a tremendous gift to all who know him. He is authentic, kind, funny, and passionately committed to walking with others to help them find Christ. My hope and prayer for you is that this book will inspire you and equip you to walk well, walk slowly, and walk intentionally with others to help them in their walk with Jesus."

—Pete Baker, co-senior leader, Life Church Lancashire, UK

"This real, honest, thought-provoking book is packed full of wisdom told through the power of personal story—the stories of those who have gone before and the greatest story ever told, the Bible. *Parallel Faith* is not just another book on discipleship but an opportunity to reflect on your own journey and consider how you can help others on theirs. Dave doesn't just teach about parallel faith, he lives it, which is why this book is a must-read."

**—Matt Brown, founder and national director,
Reality Youth Project, UK**

"*Parallel Faith* delves into discipleship by prioritizing walking alongside others on their journey to Christ. Dave has developed an intricate road map that allows each person to pull from their personal gifts in discipling others. This book sets up the reader to succeed in the God-given privilege of not only leading others to Christ but also discipling them to go and do likewise."

—Gayla Congdon, founder, Amor Ministries
—Scott Congdon, founder, Encourager

"Dave Boden's work overflows with refreshing reminders that as an apprentice to Jesus, you have something to offer that no algorithm can: 'genuine human connection, care, and understanding.' He brilliantly and practically offers tools for meaningful and authentic connections with others and for 'approaching life with a sense of inquisitiveness rooted in awe and wonder.' *Parallel Faith* offers guidance for creating caring relationships that offer opportunities to explore what God is really like in safe spaces. Prepare to have your paradigms shifted in unexpected ways by the truth that 'loving the person in front of you can indeed be done on any schedule.' If you've been looking for a guidebook for effective and sincere discipleship, you've found it!"

—Juni Felix, author and radio host,
Stanford Behavior Design Lab Teaching Team

"As church communities around the globe flounder with the struggle to be relevant and sustainable, I truly believe that the way forward is disciple-making congregations. In his book *Parallel Faith*, Boden paints a picture of a discipleship path that will prove valuable for anyone who wishes to consider how to engage in disciple-making in a practical way."

—Rev. Leanne Friesen, lead pastor,
Mount Hamilton Baptist Church, Canada

"Dave has the amazing privilege of respectfully understanding the culture of approximately 10,000 teenagers in secular education, bringing an appropriate Christian perspective to their experience. This is evidenced in how he leads us to grapple with the issue of our own disciple-making effectiveness. Parallel Faith is a powerfully helpful book that enables me to be better equipped to share my faith in post-Christian Britain, and in ways that make sense to the Jesus who asks me to share my faith with those who need me to do so. It was an enormous privilege to read a book I would gladly buy and pass on."

—John Fudge, CEO, Amor Europe

"*Parallel Faith* encourages us all to see that disciple-making is possible and powerful. Dave inspires and provokes us to see that step by step and side by side, we can see Jesus work in and through us all. Dave's inspiring honesty moves us in one moment and make us laugh in the next. May it bless and boldly challenge many."

—Amy Summerfield, CEO, Kyria Network, Head of development,
Skylark International, Zeo Church, Hitchen, UK

"There are lots of books on evangelism and lots of books on discipleship, but I love how my friend Dave Boden fuses evangelism and discipleship in this brilliant book. It is both challenging and inspiring, practical and doable, biblical and personal. Even if you don't feel you have much time to read, *Parallel Faith* is written in such a way that it can be easily read in short sessions. Honestly, this is a must-read for any follower of Jesus, however long you have been on the journey."

—Rev. Mark Greenwood, national evangelist and head of evangelism, Elim Churches UK

"A must-read for every Christian! Dave has a unique and light-hearted way of writing and inspiring all of us to take the path of intentionality when it comes to connecting and walking with others and leading them one step closer to Christ. This book helps us all rethink how we can be a positive influence and connect with others with open hearts and curious minds. It is God's work, and we are all called to play a part in it."

—Jo Haaijer, European director, OneHope

"In this book, Dave Boden offers us an accessible and inspiring opportunity to take a deep breath and reset both the purpose and trajectory of our lives. As he puts it, 'Proximity changes perspective.' In a culture constantly clamoring for more 'reach' and increased 'platform,' Boden reminds us that the greatest missional impact to be made is right here in the relationships of possibility and promise in our midst."

—Jay Y. Kim, lead pastor, WestGate Church, San Jose, California, Teacher-in-residence, Vintage Faith Church, Santa Cruz, California, Author of *Analog Christian: Cultivating Contentment, Resilience, and Wisdom in the Digital Age*

"There is such a deep need in our world for disciple-makers and insight into how we journey with people through transformational moments. Dave Boden has done a wonderful job of equipping all of us to change lives. *Parallel Faith* is a profoundly relevant, passionately winsome, and stylishly eloquent step-by-step guide of how we can make lifelong disciples of Jesus. I'm grateful for my friend's contribution to this important area of life and ministry."

—Phil Knox, evangelism and missiology, senior specialist, Evangelical Alliance, Author of *The Best of Friends: Choose Wisely, Care Well*

"This book isn't just a nice reflection of how Jesus wants to do life with others; it's an inspiring example of how the author himself has been walking alongside others on the road to Christ for years. Life is done better together, and Dave Boden is someone that anyone would love to have on their journey."

—Dan Randall, YxYA director, HOPE Together

"In the same way Jesus used parables to demystify the kingdom of God, Dave Boden has written *Parallel Faith* in such a way to demystify what is often *perceived* as more complicated than it really is: discipleship. In doing so, Boden draws and equips the everyday follower of Jesus toward Jesus' compelling vision for all of his followers to join him in his disciple-making work, right where they live."

—Alice Matagora, leader development, The Navigators, Author of *How to Save the World: Disciplemaking Made Simple*

"If you're looking for a fresh approach to disciple-making and evangelism, Dave Boden's book is for you. It's filled with great stories, current research, and biblical principles. Boden takes a subject that is profusely written about and brings new insights and new approaches. You won't find nice concepts here but practical principles and how-tos drawn from real life that will empower you to engage with people relationally and biblically where you live, work, or play."

—Bill Mowry, author of *The Ways of the Alongsider: Growing Disciples Life to Life*

"The church has a desperate need for more voices like Dave Boden's—those who are helping us understand how the people around us typically come to faith, showing us how to draw others to Jesus as we pace alongside them rather than push or pull. I cannot commend *Parallel Faith* highly enough! Dave's clear, compelling, and practical guidance feels like a friend whose encouragement gets you excited to share your faith again in everyday interactions as it guides you each step of the way."

—Darin Stevens, director, Start to Stir, Bicester, UK Author of *The Stir Course*

"*Parallel Faith* is a must-read for anyone who is passionate about Jesus and longs to see his life reproduced in and through them. Dave writes with an inspiring and a practical blend of wisdom, humour, challenge, and honesty, provoking every Christ-follower to rethink disciple-making in a way that is accessible, achievable, and powerful. May this bucketload of truth-bombs explode good news to everybody you meet."

—Matt Summerfield, senior pastor, Zeo Church, Hitchen, UK

"Practical and powerful discipleship tools from a real disciple-maker. For years, I've wished that every Christian could see how Dave and Leah Boden disciple those around them. With this book, now they can. I have learned more about living life alongside others as a Jesus follower from Dave than any other individual. He has walked beside me for much of my life following Jesus—and now through this book, he gets to walk beside you too."

—David Bowden, executive director, Spoken Gospel

Parallel
FAITH

WALKING
ALONGSIDE OTHERS
ON THEIR JOURNEY
TO CHRIST

DAVE BODEN

HENDRICKSON
PUBLISHERS

an imprint of Hendrickson Publishing Group

Parallel Faith: Walking Alongside Others on Their Journey to Christ

© 2023 Dave Boden

Published by Hendrickson Publishers
an imprint of Hendrickson Publishing Group
Hendrickson Publishers, LLC
P. O. Box 3473
Peabody, Massachusetts 01961-3473
www.hendricksonpublishinggroup.com
ISBN 978-1-4964-8347-8

Published in association with Pape Commons, www.papecommons.com.

All Scripture quotations, unless otherwise indicated, are taken from the Holy Bible, New International Version®, NIV®. Copyright ©1973, 1978, 1984, 2011 by Biblica, Inc.™ Used by permission of Zondervan. All rights reserved worldwide. www.zondervan.comThe "NIV" and "New International Version" are trademarks registered in the United States Patent and Trademark Office by Biblica, Inc.™

Scripture quotations marked (AMP) are taken from the Amplified Bible, Copyright © 2015 by The Lockman Foundation. Used by permission.

Scripture quotations marked MSG are taken from *THE MESSAGE*, copyright © 1993, 2002, 2018 by Eugene H. Peterson. Used by permission of NavPress. All rights reserved. Represented by Tyndale House Publishers, a Division of Tyndale House Ministries.

Printed in the United States of America

First Printing — September 2023

CONTENTS

INTRODUCTION

Follow my example, as I follow the example of Christ.

1 Corinthians 11:1

Just off the beautiful Mull of Kintyre Peninsula in Scotland is the secluded Davaar Island, accessible only by foot at low tide. What makes this place so unique is that the rugged shoreline hides seven mysterious caves. Each one is explorable by those willing to relive their childhood adventures and who can judge their timing's right. Davaar is a place teeming with wildlife. Otters, seabirds, and eagles can be spotted alongside dolphins, whales, and even the occasional basking shark. It is also an area of Britain rich in spiritual heritage, where ancient saints tell us ancient stories.

There is one such tale that has always fascinated me. In 1887, a local man named Archibald MacKinnon had a vivid dream in which God instructed him to paint an image of Christ in a cave on Davaar. MacKinnon then worked in secret, traveling back and forth over several weeks, painting directly onto the cave wall. When the final detailed image of Christ was first discovered by the local townsfolk, a great excitement gripped them all, as it convinced them this was a sign from God.

Visitors flocked from all over Scotland and beyond to visit this holy sight. But the delighted crowds soon became a baying mob when someone discovered that a mere mortal had created it. Rather than celebrating his artistry and innovation, the townsfolk exiled MacKinnon indefinitely!

I first heard this story while on a family holiday in the area and was determined to see the painting for myself. On a fine sunny day, the six of us set off across the sandy causeway that led to the island, trying to navigate the shifting tides. I knew I would need a guide to help me find the icon, so I had researched a travel blog that would walk me step by step through the entire journey: Turn left at this large rock here; pass the lighthouse over there; don't go too far past the lookout point. The Crucifixion Cave, as it is known, was the last of seven sea caves that ring the southern shore.

My wife, Leah, and I, along with all four of our children—Nyah, Joel, Micah, and Sienna-Raine—weaved in and out of the damp mossy caverns, counting them down until at last we came to cave number seven. Six pairs of eyes darted around at every darkened rock face as we rushed inside the triangular-shaped cavern to find the big reveal. But within minutes, the sounds of joy and glee turned to grumbles and complaints. Having scoured every inch of the cave walls, we had a growing sense of frustration in not finding what we were looking for.

Where on earth was Jesus?

We must have stepped in and out of that cave at least ten times, but Christ was nowhere to be seen. My children became disengaged and were ready to start the long coastal trek back before the tide came in. I was deeply confused, wondering where I had missed a vital instruction. And then, just as I was about to give up, I rechecked the guide and returned into the cave to take another look at a large open space just inside the entrance.

Suddenly, there he was.

A shaft of light hit a slanting rock in just the right way, and I saw his face. His arms were outstretched on his fragile body that held onto a wooden cross against a blue-tinted sky. I had been in that place before but somehow missed what was right in front of me.

I finally saw Jesus.

How on earth had I missed the one who had so obviously been there all along?

Seeing Christ for the first time felt nothing short of wondrous, and it was a holy moment for us all. But I never imagined he would be that hard to find, even when I had been told where to look. Without that guide, there was absolutely no chance I would have ever found him.

After that experience in Scotland, I have had a nagging concern that has stayed with me ever since: What if the people in our world can't find the real Jesus even when they've been told where to look? Who are the guides willing to help others discover Jesus amid all the darkness?

That's what this book is all about. I want to call us to recapture the simplicity of becoming those who walk with others until they discover Jesus from their starting point and not ours. It asks the pressing question: Do we point people in the vague direction of Jesus and then hope they can find him on their own, or are we willing to walk with them side by side on the journey?

Walking Parallel with People

All around us, there are people who don't yet know what it is like to have seen Jesus for who he really is. They are still waiting for their holy moment.

- There are those who are searching for something but don't know what they're looking for.

- Some have been looking for so long that they've given up trying altogether.

- Many had a glimpse of what they thought was Jesus only to be disappointed by yet another false impression.

- Others have been to where they thought they would find him, but they were so hurt that they may never go back there again.

If only there was one who would walk alongside them and point the way.

The word *parallel* comes from the Greek *parallēlos,* which consists of *para* meaning "alongside" and *allēlos* meaning "one another." There are fifty-nine verses in the Bible that speak to the idea of *one-anothering.* While these speak primarily to our efforts within the church community, they also point to how we ought to behave with everyone. We ought not to restrict the command to love one another to an exclusive club. Loving others means being near them.

Jesus' approach was consistently up close and personal, walking with everyone from Pharisees to prostitutes, tax collectors to fishermen, friend to foe. The secret to helping any person encounter Jesus today lies in the potency of our proximity. Jesus didn't stay in his holy huddle. As John 1:14 reads in the Message Bible,

> The Word became flesh and blood, and moved into the neighborhood.

Christ modeled for us incarnationally what it means to leave the security blanket of heaven for the sake of the world. Like Jesus, we are called to leave the comfort of our own space.

Proximity changes our perspective. We are much less likely to stereotype those from a different culture, generation, or even faith if we actually know a person from that background. This also works both ways. If a person outside the church gets to know a Christian, they are much more likely to overcome their barriers or hang-ups about Christianity.

Being present provokes empathy. If you know someone who has overcome an addiction or dealt with a major life trauma, then you are more likely to have compassion for them. When we hear of a terrible incident in our immediate neighborhood, it hits harder than if it took place on the other side of the world. The closer we are, the more connected we feel.

Proximity also invokes intimacy. According to scientific research,[1] students who sit near one another in a classroom or colleagues who work next to each other in an office statistically become better friends. There is a link between the time people spend together and the level of closeness they develop.

Let's start by considering our personal proximity problem. Ask yourself: Who do I have in my life outside of my religious bubble?

The Christian life is about walking with Jesus and walking with people. We can walk with people through their conflicts, their chaos, and their celebrations. All the while, we can point to Christ as our source of hope and love others deeply, even if they don't see Jesus in the same way we do. I am not a huge fan of the phrase "friendship evangelism" as it implies that we might use our relationships with others merely as a recruitment tactic. Nobody likes a hidden agenda. How about just friendship? Consent in relationships is the foundation of trust. Permission is a key to mission. Being clear and confident about who you are, what you stand for, and what your intentions are is all part of building a healthy connection with others.

I like the idea of a being on a shared journey. As you walk parallel with Jesus, your friends, colleagues, neighbors, and wider spheres of influence can see the benefits of a consistent lifestyle of faith, hope, and love. This is about both *showing* and *telling*. You are not developing friendships dependent on a particular set of outcomes. You just love people. And you let them love you too.

Unexpectedly, we can find an example of this kind of consistent relationship in the life of a world-famous celebrity. In a post-lockdown *GQ* article, we discover Justin Bieber's low point during one of the toughest seasons in his life. Walking with him during this time was well-known pastor Judah Smith, who refused to let go of hope on Bieber's behalf. The *GQ* article describes that anticipated breakthrough:

> When Bieber finally began to emerge from his bad years and to seek guidance, Smith was still there. And Bieber noticed that, in retrospect, Smith had never asked him for anything. "He put our relationship first," Bieber says. And then he started to notice other things, too, like the way Smith's family seemed to care for one another. "It was something I always dreamed of because my family was broken," Bieber says. "My whole life, I had a broken

family. And so I was just attracted to a family that eats dinners together, laughs together, talks together."[2]

In this snapshot, we see the importance of walking with people even when they seem far from desiring any engagement with God. Smith was *still there.* That's the key. He left ajar the door of their relationship. This story inspires me to pray that God will help me be there for others and become that nonanxious presence and the nonjudgmental advocate we often wish we had for ourselves. It's about consistently walking parallel with purpose and parallel with people, no matter where they're at.

When a person explores faith alongside us, they're not just making big decisions about God, they're making micro decisions about us. As someone tries to figure out where Jesus is, they often watch our lives closely and ask questions such as:

- Do I trust this person?
- Can I be open with them?
- What difference does *their* God make to them?
- Do I want what they have?
- Do they care about me?

Authentic, vulnerable relationships are foundational to helping those who don't know Jesus to move from a place of being uninterested to becoming spiritually curious. It's rare that we can delegate this process to a celebrity Christian or a pastor on a screen or a stage from afar. The name of the game is *connection.* God wants you to be confident to walk alongside people and help them start a journey with Jesus.

Although not everyone in your life will want to listen to your message, follow your example, or even become a Christian, that doesn't mean you can't love them. This is not about living with a hidden agenda marked by manipulation, coercion, or trickery. You don't have to be pushy or odd. It's about being honest about who you are and sharing the hope you have as you care about those around you.

Parallel with Purpose and People

The purpose of God for the church is that we go into all the world and make disciples. This was Jesus' last message and it's never needed a modern upgrade. A study by Lifeway Research[3] found that 80 percent of those who attend church one or more times a month believe they have a personal responsibility to share their faith, but 61 percent of them hadn't shared the gospel with another person in the previous six months. This is a sign that we're not quite aligned with God's purpose despite our good intentions.

Either we don't really understand the good news or we don't really have anyone to share it with. When it comes to reaching *your* world, you have to be in it to win it. There are many illustrative verses in Scripture that encourage us not to be isolated, abstracted, or excluded from the world in order to make an impact. Let's take a whistle-stop tour of just three of them.

VERSE 1: WE ARE LIKE LIGHT

"Neither do people light a lamp and put it under a bowl. Instead they put it on its stand, and it gives light to everyone in the house." (Matt. 5:15)

God does not intend for us to be hidden, tucked away, or distant. In fact, it's a malfunction of purpose to not let lights shine. For us not to be visible to those around us would be both an abdication of responsibility and a dimming of our destiny. Yes, Jesus is the light of the world, but the plan of God was to put that light inside a community of people who would then reveal it to others. The whole of church history is like the lighting of heaven's Olympic torch that now rests in our hands, ready to pass on.

VERSE 2: WE ARE LIKE SALT

"You are the salt of the earth. But if salt loses its saltiness, how can it be made salty again?" (Matt. 5:13)

Here, Jesus uses salt as an analogy to show that Christians can add value and flavor to the world around them. This is not because we are better than anyone else, but because we have Jesus with us, in us, and working through us. Yet the verse also comes with a warnying not to lose that sense of saltiness—namely, the integrity of who we are. As we live in proximity with those around us, it's vital we stay close to Christ and keep him as our way, truth, and life. We are both inclusive and distinctive.

Verse 3: God's Kingdom Is Like Yeast

"The kingdom of heaven is like yeast that a woman took and mixed into about sixty pounds of flour until it worked all through the dough." (Matt. 13:33)

Jesus uses yeast here as an illustration, referring to how something small and seemingly insignificant can highly influence the environment in which it's embedded. You can't be an influencer if you live your life at arm's length. This is why Jesus had the biggest open-door policy of anyone. He was like that yeast: he infiltrated everywhere!

When we think of words like *evangelism*, we often default to the stereotype of a loud preacher standing on a street corner, banging on a door with tracts, or trying to fill a stadium for an event. This approach often perpetuates a sense of *us* and *them* and keeps others at arm's length. But what if evangelism is about walking alongside others and letting our words and deeds shine through? By the way we live for, speak about, and point to Jesus, we can proclaim the good news in our daily lives. We can all make disciples and fulfill God's mission whoever we are and whatever we do. You don't have to be in full-time ministry in the church to be in full-time ministry with God!

This is what it means to be *parallel with purpose.*

In the same way, *discipleship* is another buzz-word that has been pigeon-holed to structured programs led by pastors, preachers, or professionals. We tend to think it is about following a set method, in a fixed way, at a specific time. This leaves little room for the normal average Christian who doesn't feel qualified enough. But what if discipleship is actually walking alongside anyone to help them take a small step toward Jesus from any starting point?

This is what it means to be *parallel with people*.

In some ways, it's hard to distinguish where evangelism ends and discipleship starts when we think of walking with others as both begin from different stages of a spectrum. I love the way Alan Hirsch combined these concepts through the term "discipism." He describes mission like an ongoing journey:

> By simply following the Great Commission literally, we begin to see that conversion is a process that begins right at the start of the journey towards Jesus! Listen to what I'm saying here: Discipleship should start even before people become regenerated ("born-again") converts and continue right till the end.[4]

Let me be clear that I'm not trying to say that one type or style of mission is better than another. God can use anyone by any means. Jesus constantly changed his methods but was always driven by one motive: love.

You don't need to be a certain personality type or have any special training to walk side by side with others. You just need to be available. In being parallel with people, you don't have to be perfect, but you do have to be present.

Although investing a lot of time in people requires a huge amount of focus, attention, and energy, it's what really works for being effective in fulfilling God's purpose for the world. In the words of author Pete Scazzero:

> If you're going to be serious about discipleship, you're going to go the same way as Jesus. It's going to be sloppy, difficult, messy, small, and slow. That's it. You're going to have to figure out, "How am I going to disciple a few?"[5]

By understanding more about the process of how people come to Christ over time, I believe you will feel more empowered to play your part in leading anyone to take one more step toward Jesus. What a brilliant adventure that can be.

As you think about the power of proximity,

- *Can you identify the names of people you're already walking alongside in your daily life who wouldn't yet call themselves followers of Jesus?*

- *How are you praying for them right now?*

PART ONE

PARALLEL WITH PURPOSE

In this first section of the book, we focus on *why* it is so important to start walking alongside others on their journey to Christ. Thinking about evangelism and discipleship as a continual spectrum empowers us to help others take steps toward Jesus from any starting point. In thinking about being *parallel with purpose,* we will learn that:

✓ Every church has a cause.

✓ Every person has a process.

✓ Every believer has a bubble.

✓ Every disciple has a destination.

✓ Every soul can be stirred.

✓ Every excuse can be eliminated.

✓ Every mindset can be missional.

1

WALKING

A voice of one is calling out, "Clear the way for the Lord in the wilderness [remove the obstacles]; Make straight and smooth in the desert a highway for our God."

Isaiah 40:3 (AMP)

My jaw almost dropped to the floor when I noticed a teenager called Sarah walk into our church for the first time. I honestly thought she had come to the wrong building by mistake! Whereas many school students I knew wouldn't have known what the label "atheist" meant, Sarah would define herself as one. While outwardly I perceived her as almost militant in her antireligious views, I didn't know she had inwardly been on her own secret journey with Jesus and had decided it was time to check out church for herself.

I first met Sarah through my work in a local school, where we educated students about the basics of Christian belief without ever crossing the line into proselytizing. Education is about giving people the tools to explore subjects for themselves. When we came to Christianity in Religious Education lessons, I realized that a lot of the young people like Sarah simply didn't have any prior awareness of the topic at hand. They had not grown up in a family where faith was discussed, and nine out of ten had never been to a church meeting in their life. Their knowledge was at a level you could visualize as like fresh snow without footprints.

I recently reminisced with Sarah about her transformation since leaving school. She had become a Christian and joined our local church community, even after she had initially so publicly rejected Christ.

"How long have we known you now, Sarah?" I said after we finished a small group Bible study my wife was leading.

"I first met you when I was twelve," she responded with a grin on her face. "That seems like only yesterday to me."

"And remind me how old you are now?" I asked, pretending I already knew the answer.

"I'm twenty-eight," said the twelve-year-old.

Sixteen years had passed in the blink of an eye, and like so many, Sarah's journey to Jesus had started far beyond the walls of the local church, taking many twists and turns along the way.

I am always fascinated by the markers that define a person's spiritual walk before they decide to follow Jesus. It's often the little things that made the difference. For Sarah, it was the opportunity to explore God in a safe space, the chance to have conversations and make connections, and that she could argue with people like me and know I wouldn't give up on her. Even after she crossed the threshold of a church, she still had a journey before her. We often miss this process in our keenness to tick the attendance box, as if sitting in a pew is the same as fulfilling a purpose.

Over the years, I have had the wonderful privilege of helping many people make their first moves toward freedom, destiny, and belonging with Jesus. Some people start their journey after a significant conversation with a Christian—whether a mentor, relative, or friend. Others stumble onto something while scrolling on the internet that helps them find good news amid fake news. Sometimes a moment of crisis brings a wake-up call or an answered prayer comes in the middle of a storm.

Every person has to come to that point of responding yes or no to the invitation from Jesus to follow him. Even if you've been raised in a home full of Christians, you still have to make a choice to follow Christ for yourself. Everyone has to take little steps toward Jesus before they can take big steps with him.

The Chronicles of Lewis

In the movie *The Most Reluctant Convert,* based on the play of the same name, we see an in-depth example of one man's personal pathway to finding faith. Thinking about the story of Clive Staples Lewis, I'm always struck by how long the lead time to conversion was for him. During a kneeling prayer in 1929 when he finally succumbed to the idea that there even was a God, it's said that it took a further twelve years for him to give in to following Christ.

In one of his letters to a friend, Lewis writes about that night of significance:

> You must picture me alone in that room in Magdalen, night after night, feeling, whenever my mind lifted even for a second from my work, the steady, unrelenting approach of Him whom I so earnestly desired not to meet. That which I greatly feared had at last come upon me. In the Trinity Term of 1929 I gave in, and admitted that God was God, and knelt and prayed: perhaps, that night, the most dejected and reluctant convert in all of England.[1]

C. S. Lewis embraced a slow-burner approach toward following Jesus—perhaps because he knew what an authentic yes to God was going to cost him. Though he attended church as a child with his strict father, he was out the door as soon as he had the chance. Through many years of study, he cemented a staunch atheist viewpoint. Yet he soon wrestled with his own unbelief as his friends, the books he read, and his personal experience of God pulling on his heart influenced him. In his book *Surprised by Joy,* Lewis describes this as being hunted down, as if God was a hunter and he was a deer.

Sometimes it feels like God is happier to play the long game than we are.

I recently took a stroll on the legendary Addison's Walk, which is part of Magdalen College at Oxford University, where Lewis was a faculty member. In September 1941, Lewis, the famous J. R. R. Tolkien, and their friend Hugo Dyson took a formative journey one night along that same loop. The discussions that took place became instrumental in Lewis's decision-making process. On that day, it's said they talked about everything from "metaphor to myth"; and in Lewis's retelling to his friend Arthur Greeves, the conversation that started on Addison's Walk lasted well into the early hours of the morning:

> We continued (in my room) on Christianity: a good long satisfying talk in which I learned a lot: then discussed the difference between love and friendship—then finally drifted back to poetry and books.[2]

The next day, Lewis decided that Jesus was a reality worth following. In that conversation on Addison's Walk, strongholds must have been broken, barriers removed, eyes opened, and hearts softened. If it wasn't for that long walk, perhaps we would never have known the legacy of Lewis in the same way we do today. Maybe he would have been just another scholar destined for obscurity?

Addison's Walk is a quintessentially English looped path that parallels the Oxford Canal. Designed for human connection, there is just enough space for two people to walk side by side. On the day that I walked that same path in the balmy Oxford sun, I imagined I was walking with Lewis, Dyson, and Tolkien, and I strained to listen to the lingering conversations of history. I had an epiphany that when we think about discipleship, we ought to picture it as walking side by side with people, leading them toward an encounter with Christ.

To journey parallel with people is to explore with them, to be curious, to listen, to allow space for questions, and not to rush a single step. Life so often sets up stumbling blocks, diversions, distractions, or "no entry" signs for those seeking God. Our role is to partner with God to help create a straighter path for people to encounter Jesus in their own lives. This is what it means to prepare the way. Right from the get-go, we have to release ourselves from any expectation of being responsible for the ultimate outcome. You do your part and let God do his. We are not the rescuers.

What was it that helped clear the way for Lewis? The art of conversation played a fundamental role in him taking small steps toward Christ. While he could take a walk of enquiry with friends, how quick are we to hurry people down our religious conveyor belt? I wonder where the safe spaces are for this kind of dynamic dialogue during our busy church culture today? The question for us now is whether we still have the patience to walk with others in this process.

As well as conversation, it was creativity that played a key role in preparing the way for Lewis's commitment to Christ. The work of the Scottish author, poet, and minister George MacDonald moved Lewis. As a pioneer in fantasy literature, MacDonald became a tremendous influence on Lewis's style long before he created the world of Narnia. If creativity like this can move people toward Christ, then we ought to ask, Where are the modern George MacDonalds today? Who is creating content that engages people beyond the confines of the church? Or is all of our creative effort still serving those inside our church walls?

C. S. Lewis was not someone who would have made an impulsive choice to be influenced by an inspiring speaker, bright lights, and video screens, or emotional soft piano and guitar music. His conviction came from a raw encounter with the God who had been wooing him even as he had been challenging him to count the cost. When you look closely at Lewis's life, there are a series of events, nudges, opportunities, and moments that remind us what the side-by-side journey looks like. You may even call this evolutionary unfolding *pre-discipleship*. More on that word later.

The Journey toward Jesus

Imagine for a moment you're watching a television show like *Dragons' Den* for the Brits or *Shark Tank* for the Americans. You see the usual mixed bag of pitches for pointless inventions like virtual reality for pets, wax-melt candles made from yak's milk, or a business that sells pumpkins to people in the summer so they can get ahead of the autumn rush. Suddenly, the voiceover unexpectedly announces that the next two pitches will feature special guests from the Christian community on church growth. You lean in to pay attention to see what happens next.

> *Pitch 1.* An impressive leader dressed in a brand-new suit comes out and outlines his plans for church growth. It centers on greater profiling of his personality, running an amazing teaching program, hiring a high-performance marketing team, and executing his professional plan for content creation and distribution across the entire city.
>
> The investors are amazed and instantly give the leader all the money he asks for.
>
> *Pitch 2.* Next up, dressed in casual clothes, Jesus comes out before the investors and outlines his plans for church growth. He says, "I want to take a small group of people and intentionally journey with them for a few years. I'm going to invest my life into them, love them, and lead them into a life of sacrifice that will forever affect eternity. And I don't even need a building or a budget to do it."
>
> The investors are quick to declare that it will never work, and one by one they say, "I'm out!"

You can see why the investors would appreciate the first pitch more: It offers tangible and measurable signs of impact. You can always gather a crowd behind a charismatic personality and culturally relevant message. The Jesus approach seems inherently riskier on first impression. It feels like a huge long-term investment.

Although you'd never logically think that Jesus' plan would work, it already has.

This model of slow, side-by-side spiritual transformation from the inside out has been working for over two thousand years, driven by the engine of God's Holy Spirit. Our challenge today is that we have taken something organic and tried to manufacture it on a mass scale. It sometimes feels like our strategy to grow our churches goes something like this:

- Work hard to get lots of people to attend meetings and programs.

- Consume people's time, energy, and effort to keep those meetings and programs running efficiently.

- Send the crowd we gather out to get more people to attend meetings and programs.

Jesus, however, modeled something radically different for us to consider if we are to follow in his footsteps:

- Take a few people and walk with them from day one.

- Help empower those people to disciple others.

- Impact the world as we walk side by side together with him.

Why then is our emphasis too often still on recruiting people to a program rather than leading them on a journey? Perhaps this is because small movements are rarely as exciting as giant leaps. If faith formation is more transitional, gradual, and relational than we think, then it's important to question why our methods are often reduced to being transactional, impersonal, and locked into the confines of a church building. As one church strategist puts it, "Even though our spiritual journeys don't begin when we put our trust in Jesus, most churches act like they do."[3]

Let's be honest, Christians often jump the gun and try to *seal the deal* with people way too early. This is often down to our desire to see temporary visible results rather than eternal impact. This happens when we see people as targets to sign up to our club rather than souls who need a savior.

It's important that we see discipleship not just as a destination but as a pathway. This is not so we can get more people to attend our church meetings. It's because God wants us to walk parallel with his purpose. What if the next person you meet is another C. S. Lewis waiting for you to invite them to take a stroll on Addison's Walk?

REFLECT ═══

When you consider your own journey of how you came to Christ,

- *What were the significant moments or stages you had to take before you became a Christian?*

- *How would you lay out these steps on a timeline if you had to decode them for others?*

2

GOING

"Come, follow me," Jesus said, "and I will
send you out to fish for people."

Matthew 4:19

Back in the early 2000s, the British government became increasingly concerned about the dietary habits of the nation and wanted to get people eating their greens again. The "5 a Day" slogan was launched by the Department of Health and backed by an extensive TV and radio advertising campaign aimed at increasing personal fruit and vegetable intake to five portions a day. So popular and pervasive was the "5 a Day" motto that it became one of the best-known pieces of advice of all time and is still widely used today.

Yet problems with the "5 a Day" campaign's effectiveness soon emerged. As public awareness exploded, levels of behavior change stagnated. While everyone now knew the importance of eating more fruit and vegetables, they still ignored it. In fact, a decade after the slogan had taken root in popular culture, the overall consumption of fruit and vegetables continued to decline. Some still call this the most successful failed marketing of all time.

Here's the thing: Just because we all know something doesn't mean we do anything about it.

I often think about this when I consider one of the most famous verses in the Bible found in Matthew 28:18–20.

> Then Jesus came to them and said, "All authority in heaven and
> on earth has been given to me. Therefore go and make disciples
> of all nations, baptizing them in the name of the Father and of
> the Son and of the Holy Spirit, and teaching them to obey every-
> thing I have commanded you. And surely I am with you always,
> to the very end of the age."

We all know the command given by Jesus is to *make disciples*. But
if we are honest, some of us seem to do very little to prioritize it in
our everyday lives. The gap between knowledge and action is stark.
God did not mean that *making disciples* was an optional extra for
Christians to fit into their otherwise busy church schedules. This
exciting adventure was never meant to be a task for the professionals, but one where all team members play their part out on the field.

Make disciples ought to be Christianity's version of Nike's "Just
Do It." It should permeate everything we do and be instantly recognizable as our mantra. Yet if we look at the declining statistics on faith formation, or at the rising concerns about church
disengagement, then we might have to conclude that things are
not going as well as we had hoped in the whole discipleship department. The number of people calling themselves practicing
Christians in the United States has dropped in half since 2000.[1]
Research tells us that in every age category, weekly church attendance has dropped over the past twenty years and declined
even further since the global pandemic.

Even if you are a churchgoer, one recent survey concluded 70
percent of "born again" Christians now believe that Jesus Christ
isn't the only way to God.[2] It's no wonder that amid these challenges, we're not winning with the next generation. Ninety-five
percent of young people in the UK are not connected to any local
church community,[3] and in North America, two-thirds of young
Christians who went to church as teens stop attending right after
high school.[4]

From Hounslow to Houston, we have a problem.

On their own, these shocking statistics don't offer a full scientific analysis of the issue. It's worth stating from the onset that
being a church attender, or even someone who believes in God,

are not always the same thing as being a disciple. If you think about it, we have billions of believers already. As Church of England priest Cris Rogers says,

> At its heart, the church has to be disciple making, not just believer making. Jesus is not just looking for more believers, he is also looking for people who will give everything of themselves to His mission to change the world.[5]

Without a clear focus on a vision for discipleship, the church often ends up with lots of believers and very few disciples. Maybe that's why so many Christians get caught up in the religious hamster wheel and end up exhausting themselves with endless activities that don't seem to have any lasting impact. A major issue of mission creep seems to have emerged, especially in the Western church.

Going beyond Our Bubbles

When I was a teenager, I was desperate to set up an aquarium and create a dramatic display from which even Nemo wouldn't want to escape. Inside a well-established fish tank was a whole independent ecosystem that thrived all by itself. I watched as the colorful variety of guppies, platys, and barbs swam in endless circles of hypnotizing movement. And I delighted as the coral lived in synergy with the tiny sand creatures that I had given a home.

It takes a lot of work, but if you get the right heater, filter, and water treatment, a budding aquarium owner really can recreate their own little tropical paradise. You can even make gigantic waves inside your own fish tank. That's the theory, anyway. My youthful efforts, however, always seemed to end up with my fish mysteriously disappearing overnight. To this day, I don't know where the bubble-eyed fancy goldfish went after I lovingly wished them goodnight! It turns out that it takes an extraordinary amount of time, energy, and effort to keep the fish happy.

Introducing a new fish was a technical nightmare. First, you went to the shop and chose the type you wanted. After bringing it home, you had to undergo this long-winded ceremony, where the water in the bag they came in had to be slowly mixed with the water of your tank over a period of time. If you skipped the process and chucked the fish right in at the deep end, then you would find it sunbathing on the surface the next day. Outsiders find it hard to mix in a culture that's so different from the habitat they came from.

No matter what happens inside the aquarium, there is one fact that's always true: nothing on the outside is ever really affected by what happens on the inside. It can be wet as the ocean on the interior, but dry as a bone on the exterior. You can adjust the temperature, clean the water, add better lights, and even choose more colorful stones, but this will never change the fact that your fish are locked in their own little world.

As strange as it may sound, there is an illustration here regarding the church. So much happens inside that we forget what's happening elsewhere. Is this fishbowl mentality the reason we're struggling to fulfill the Great Commission?

Decades ago, American radio and television broadcaster Paul Harvey challenged the church in his time by saying, "We've strayed from being Fishers of Men to being keepers of the aquarium."

He used the phrase "keepers of the aquarium" to explain how such a huge investment of time, energy, and money now goes into getting our inner ecosystem right. We decorate our stages and try to make our atmosphere perfect. We attempt to be hypnotic in our displays, cycles, and rhythms in our efforts to keep the fish happy. Yet somehow, we seem to make big waves that are only ever felt in our own fishbowl. We get locked into maintenance mode.

There is something fishy going on (excuse the pun) when we become fixated with controlling the environment, making it so comfortable that no one ever really wants to leave it, and no one can easily get in without having a major experience of culture shock. This is the ocean-sized curse of being inward-looking. We can either invest our time in keeping us all comfortable, making sure our preferences are being met, and doing things our way, or we can start reaching out to others.

I am deeply committed to the church and have always felt part of it. There is great comfort to be found within the boundaries of a worshiping, loving, and praying community. I believe in the local church because God does. But the danger is that we struggle to engage beyond our own religious fishbowls.

Going Outside Our Comfort Zone

During my time as lead pastor of a local church, there was one moment that gave me insight into where I think so many of us Christians are stationary when it comes to going. We were getting an increase in the numbers of people interested in knowing more about Jesus, and we wanted to launch a helpful training course with a difference. It was to be called *Bible Buddies*, and one of the Bible teachers in our church pulled together a set of simple teachings based around the foundations of Christianity. Rather than just telling people "God loves you," this would be a chance to examine together the actual Scriptures that speak of God's love while we walked alongside them.

The basic premise was this: If you know someone who wants to know more about Jesus, then you can coach them yourself using the ready-to-use material provided. You didn't have to wait for a program to start at a set time in a set place; there was no need to pass them off to a pastor. The motto was "each one can reach one"—anytime and anyplace. Bible Buddies was successful for a while and saw many people take up the mantle to help new believers take steps toward Jesus. We later turned it into a digital resource that is still being used today.

But some of the feedback we received at the time of launch sidestepped me considerably. Several responses to Bible Buddies ranged from "I don't really have time to help anyone learn about Jesus," to "I am already involved in serving elsewhere in the church." Others said, "I don't feel qualified to disciple someone myself," or more worryingly, "No one ever did this for me."

Many had been in churches for years, but they didn't feel equipped or empowered to do the one thing that Jesus taught us should be our number one priority. In that season, I learned that the answer to creating a disciple-making culture is about more than just providing a program. It's about changing a mindset.

This is where the gap between the church and culture can become as grand as a canyon. On the one hand, we have this world where people are desperate for good news and long to find answers to the most important questions of their life. On the other hand, there's a church community that doesn't quite know how to move the dial when it comes to discipleship.

What if society is looking for answers that the church doesn't feel adequately equipped to give?

If this is even half true, then it raises urgent questions about how we really prioritize the mandate to make disciples. Jesus told us that the harvest is plenty, but the workers are few. This means we have a human resource issue, not a heavenly one. But I believe there is a deep desire in Christians who want more than this. They see what is happening beyond our church walls and yearn to make a difference. They hear the same call as the ancient prophet Isaiah and have said, "Here I am, send me."

Going Right Where You Are

I was about fourteen years old at a youth camp meeting when I heard a preacher, Jonny Matthew, make an invitation for us to become missional that somehow worked its way into my soul: "I don't just want to see this place filled with the same old faces next year. I want to see this room filled with the lost and the broken young people from your school and your neighborhood." I'm not sure what it was about these words—but on reflection, it was perhaps the first time in my life I realized that the good news of Jesus wasn't only for me. On that day, I first said my own feeble version of "Okay, God, then send me." It was more of a whisper than a courageous shout. I believe the Holy Spirit caused something to stir in me, and it triggered a lifelong agitation that we can't stay in our Christian bubble.

After that, I felt compelled to tell others about Jesus even while I was still trying to figure out how to live the Christian life myself. It was scary, and I didn't feel like I was equipped or good enough to help others. Yet, enough was changing in me to be inspired to get involved in outreach in a tough neighborhood as a teenager. I'll never forget those early days of using action figures to explain the gospel to groups of young children while stones were being thrown at the community building by a gang of disruptive youths!

I later realized that you don't have to take part in an outreach activity to live life on a mission.

When it comes to "going," people often think of traveling to the far side of the world from where they live. History is full of incredible missionaries who made an impact beyond the shores of their own horizons. But you don't need a plane ticket to step out of your comfort zone. There are a thousand opportunities to make a difference right where you are, every single day.

God's mandate is about the daily decision to go into *your* world: the people and places you're already connected to in your daily life. Who are you already alongside in your family, friendships, and community groups? What connections do you have in your work and business networks? Who do you know in your neighborhood or even from your childhood? Where do you hang out and take part in your hobbies, sports, or volunteering? What's the digital footprint you're leaving behind in a sea of likes, comments, and shares?

Start where you are. Unless you live in the depths of the Antarctic, you should be able to live parallel to and in proximity with people. When you consider the circle of influence you already have, it's transformational to believe that it might not be an accident where God has placed you. Pastor Rich Villodas reminds us that the idea that God has been at work before you is vital to the mission of going:

> Good missional theology and practice believes that wherever we go, God has already been working. We don't bring God anywhere. Rather, we discover through prayer and conversation where God has been at work.[6]

You can't bring God anywhere he isn't already. Rather than think we need to be everyone's hero, we can become more like a detective who steps back, listens, and seeks God to ask what he is already doing with a person, place, or project. Instead of asking "What am *I* doing here, God?" we can ask "What are *you* doing here, God?"

An enormous shift in our thinking happens when we see that every person has a process before they come to Christ and not just afterwards. Discipleship starts on day one.

To think that discipling can take place only once someone has entered the walls of a church is almost like setting up a fishing rod in the middle of the desert and waiting for a fish to jump out of nowhere onto the bait. If this were true, then there would be no need to start the Great Commission with the word *go*.

REFLECT ===

- *To what extent do you feel you are stuck in a religious bubble right now?*

- *Where can you start to break out of your comfort zone and connect with new people?*

3

BECOMING

Whoever claims to live in him must live as Jesus did.

1 John 2:6

Back in 2015, there was a British TV commercial that was so inspiring it almost made me want to join the Royal Navy! In it, the narrator Gareth Keelor speaks in a strong regional accent about his life growing up on the edge of the Scottish borders: "Said my first word at one. Kicked off the stabilizers at four. United mad by seven. Bored at eleven."

Life goes on. Things are business as usual until he joins the Royal Navy and his life changes. Being trained, developed, and challenged by the armed forces changed everything from the inside out. Gareth was shaped by his experience in the navy for the better.

> I upped my game. Made a leap. I learned to think on my feet. I did things I never dreamed I would. And overcame things I never thought I could. The elements. The distance. The fears.

Right at the end of the promotional video, he delivers a memorable catchphrase designed to inspire potential new recruits. "Sure. I was *born* in Carlisle. But I was *made* in the Royal Navy."

This advertisement reminds us of the difference between being *born* and being *made*. All of us are born once, but then we are *made* a thousand times over.

We are formed (or deformed) by our context, background, and the challenges we face. Our life experiences, our encounters with people, and our education all constantly shape us. The media we consume forges us. Algorithms that drive our social media usage mold us. The surrounding culture wills us to conform. We exist in a state of being formed even after we are physically grown. We are all being shaped by something. As John Mark Comer says in his book *Live No Lies*,

> Spiritual formation isn't just a follower of Jesus thing; it's a human thing. We're all being formed every minute of every day. We're all becoming someone. Intentional or unintentional, conscious or unconscious, deliberate or haphazard, we're all in the process of becoming a person.[1]

A disciple is one who is being formed more by Jesus than by the world. This is God's plan: You are *born* on earth, but you are *made* by Jesus. Discipleship happens by design. We are called to be like one who is an apprentice formed by a master.

Shaped by "Churchianity"

Unfortunately, based on what we observe in the average church, we might assume that the proper goal of our spiritual formation is to get people to attend, serve, give, and even lead in our church services. We are, by default or design, working really hard to *make attendees* rather than seeking to *make disciples*. No matter what we preach or teach, the reality of our day-to-day practice speaks for itself.

Missiologist Will Mancini describes the overprogrammed and under-discipled nature of church life in his book *Future Church* stating that the functional commission of the North American church (and in other parts of the world too) has effectively become something like, "Go into all the world and make more worship attenders, baptizing them in the name of small groups and teaching them to volunteer a few hours a month."[2] If this unwritten rule is true, then it explains why we call people who don't yet know Jesus by the term "unchurched." Across Christendom, church influencers are prolifically using this adjective right now.

If our goal is to try to "churchify" people, then it's no wonder we refer to people outside our community as unchurched. To me, it is almost a subconscious way of saying, "Don't worry, guys; let's keep going with this new person and eventually we can make them 'churched' like the rest of us."

I love the local church, but I pray God will deliver us all from being *churched*. If that's the endgame, then I'm out. Nobody wants to get up in the morning and be driven by the purpose of doing more religious stuff. Jesus' vision was so much bigger than helping people get fantastic at church activities.

It's called Christianity, not churchianity.

So, according to the Bible, what does success look like for a disciple? Let's take a brief look at four key Bible verses where Jesus talks about what it actually means to be shaped as a disciple. Each one has this word *disciple* at the heart.

SHAPE 1: LEARN WITH JESUS

Jesus said, "If you hold to my teaching, you are really my disciples. Then you will know the truth, and the truth will set you free."
(John 8:31–32)

Being a disciple means learning about and with Jesus. The word *disciple* comes from the Greek *Mathetes*, which essentially means "learner-doer." A disciple is someone who wears "learner" plates; they never get their driver's license. This contrasts the church, which is often flooded with know-it-alls instead of show-it-alls.

It's easy to put the knowledge we gain into a religious box and keep it separate from our everyday life. We have all seen the T-shirt that reads, "Another day has passed, and I still haven't used algebra." Our Christian life can be like this: the knowledge we gain has no relevance to us because we never intend to put it into practice. This is why so many of us are feeling more bored-again than born-again!

We even have an education system where we like to compartmentalize learning into different subjects. But Jesus will not let us get away with compartmentalizing his teaching. If we want to be disciples, then his words must impact every part of our lives.

Humans were designed to learn as they do. Yet, we are often so full of knowledge that we don't know what to do with it. The education Jesus gives is one that fills our minds but also transforms our hearts. Life-giving truth therefore forms every true disciple. We are shaped by learning with Jesus.

SHAPE 2: LIVE FOR JESUS

Then [Jesus] said to them all: "Whoever wants to be my disciple must deny themselves and take up their cross daily and follow me. For whoever wants to save their life will lose it, but whoever loses their life for me will save it."
(Luke 9:23–24)

Being a disciple means living for Jesus and letting him lead every aspect of your life. Following him is about your whole life and not just your church life. We don't root our lives in self-improvement or self-actualization. Discipleship is not about the so-called project self. The key to following Jesus is to choose to say, "Not *my* will, but yours be done." Following Jesus means letting go of your own will, ambition, goals, and desires, and confirming to his.

In crude terms, all disciples are losers. To deny yourself is to say no to being led by your own will and no to being dictated to by the ways of the world. It's about letting Jesus shape your *lived experience*. As we do this, we discover a deeper meaning and purpose for our life.

Taking up your cross is a deliberate act of paying a price to walk with Christ. This is not exactly an appealing thing on a surface level. By our twenty-first-century standards, many would say that Jesus wasn't a very good evangelist. Whenever he seemed to gather a big crowd, he tried his hardest to talk them out of following him! Jesus was not exactly an effective marketer. That's because he wasn't offering a product; he was offering a side-by-side journey.

Submitting to Jesus forms us into disciples rather than follow-ing our own selfish ambitions. We are shaped by living for Jesus.

SHAPE 3: LOVE LIKE JESUS

"A new command I give you: Love one another. As I have loved you, so you must love one another. By this everyone will know that you are my disciples, if you love one an-other." (John 13:34–35)

Being a disciple means loving like Jesus. I remember once driv-ing on a five-hour round trip from Wales to the Midlands to see my future wife, Leah, for just one evening, making the return trip at 1:00 a.m. I was so tired on the journey back that I missed the turn for Cardiff and ran out of petrol. I will never forget walk-ing down the motorway at 3:00 a.m. with a petrol can in my hand, feeling on top of the world! People will do crazy, costly things for love.

The word *amateur* comes from a French word meaning "lover." Professionals do something out of obligation because they must fulfill a role. Amateurs do something because they love it. The church needs more amateurs! The call to disciple-ship is a call to walk in intimacy with Christ. Love sustains us on the side-by-side journey. Being loved by God means we love like God as we model the same kindness, forgiveness, gentleness, and grace we discover in Christ. Love forms a disciple. We are shaped by loving like Jesus.

SHAPE 4: LOOK LIKE JESUS

"A student is not above the teacher, but everyone who is fully trained will be like their teacher." (Luke 6:40)

Being a disciple means becoming like Jesus. In this verse in Luke, we can see that after a period of training, the student becomes like the teacher. The end goal of discipleship is always that we reflect Jesus to our world. Disciples are formed to the point where they reveal the spirit of Jesus Christ in all they do.

While on route to Zambia with a group of school students, the school trip I was leading visited Regina Mundi Church in Johannesburg on a South African layover. Despite being exhausted after a long flight, the group of students mustered up the strength to at least half-listen to the tour guide lead us around and teach us about the church's rich political history. This was a church that still had visible gunshot holes in the rafters from the anti-apartheid riots . After showing us the culturally significant *Black Madonna* painting, admired by presidents and poor people alike, our escort led us to another part of the church and showed us a hanging icon.

"Do you notice anything about that statue of Jesus on the wall there?" he asked to provoke curiosity and snap a couple of students out of their zombie-like slumber.

A small group of us patiently stood and looked for a while at the statue, as if searching for a hidden figure in a *Where's Waldo?* picture.

Suddenly, one student blurted out the correct answer. "Jesus has no hands!" she said. "Jesus has no hands!"

Instantly, I saw the statue again as if I was seeing it for the first time. The outstretched arms of Jesus had nothing beyond the wrists.

"That's right!" the tour guide responded with glee, as if the young person had just answered the ultimate question on *Who Wants to Be a Millionaire?* "Because *we* are the hands of Jesus in this world."

The image of a handless Christ in the slums of Soweto is one that has always stayed with me. It serves as a reminder that becoming like Jesus means we must become his visible hands and feet in our world.

People can't see Jesus, but they can see us.

"We are the hands of Jesus in this world." That's quite a mission statement. This is what Christlikeness is all about: being the hands and feet of Jesus. God wants to shape your life until you think, speak, and act just like Jesus, as if he were alive in *your* world today. A disciple is formed and shaped to look like Jesus.

We might sum up the whole discipleship journey in the following sentence:

> *Being a disciple is about learning, living, and loving in the context of a Jesus-centered community, with Christlikeness as the goal.*

When we know what the endgame is, we can go back to the start and build from a stronger foundation. When we see discipleship explained in this simple way, the gaps in our own church experience sometimes appear stark. Many Christians would struggle to explain how they had been discipled themselves, let alone imagine the thought of taking personal responsibility to support others to this aim. This is why we need to continually walk parallel with God's purpose as much as we walk parallel with God's people.

Spiritual formation is the ongoing process of growing more in Christlike love, joy, and peace. It is allowing God to patiently form his kindness, goodness, and gentleness in us. The incredible thing is that as we focus on our own pursuit of becoming more like Jesus, it inevitably rubs off on others. Our own formation can form others:

- Those who love like Jesus will find themselves among the last, the least, and the lost.

- Those who live in peace will stick out like a sore thumb in an anxiety-ridden world.

- Those who find joy in all circumstances will bless those who haven't yet found hope.

- Those who are not formed by the culture can form the culture itself.

If we really want people to live for Jesus, learn with Jesus, love like Jesus, and in doing so look like him, then everything else has to become secondary.

Maybe it's time for an honest assessment about where most of our time, energy, money, and efforts in church really go. Are we all about making music, social connections, and programs? Or are we about making disciples?

REFLECT ══

- *What are the main things you'd say are shaping your life right now?*

- *Consider each of these four discipleship verses about learning, living, loving, and looking:*

  > *Learning with Jesus (John 8:31–32)*

  > *Living for Jesus (Luke 9:23–24)*

  > *Loving like Jesus (John 13:34–35)*

  > *Looking like Jesus (Luke 6:40)*

- *Which of these can you relate to the most in terms of where you're at right now in your personal walk with Christ?*

- *Which do you think you need to focus on more?*

4

DISCOVERING

Jesus answered, "I am the way and the truth and the life. No one comes to the Father except through me."

John 14:6

My friend Lewis had been a Christian for about four and a half years before I got to know him and heard his story. In his past, he had lived hell-bent on chasing after the thrill of drinking, drugs, and clubbing from a young age even before he could legally do so. Lewis would have called himself an atheist with no interest in God at all. He had no church connections except for one friend, Giles, who had grown up attending a local congregation with his mum.

His unbelief in God slowly shifted when Giles came back from university and had discovered Jesus and not just religion. As Lewis spent time with Giles, there was a noticeable difference in his life. His childhood pal began sharing what he called "little testimonies" about what God was doing in his life. Lewis did not always welcome this and vividly recalls one time saying to his friend while playing on the Xbox: "Can you just shut up?! We can't even play FIFA now without you going on about Jesus!"

But somehow the little testimonies stuck.

Although Lewis would have told you he didn't yet understand the gospel, during one of the "little testimony" sessions, Giles spoke about his experience of what he called "the presence of God." Rather than put him off with the obscure language, Lewis was fascinated by the idea that you could be close to God. Something was shifting in his thinking. God was now on the agenda. Wisely, his friend didn't coerce him into deciding to become a Christian during these early conversations; rather, he encouraged him to pray and seek God for himself.

A major turning point came when Lewis prayed for a personal experience of God. This led to miraculously being delivered from a constant feeling of paranoia and finding a peace that passes all understanding. In this season, he also had a vivid dream through which the voice of God spoke to him and declared, "Those that are not worthy will not enter the kingdom of heaven." This was especially significant as there was no prior knowledge of religious language, so Lewis had to go ask Giles what the words even meant!

Soon after this, Lewis found himself at yet another party, ready for another high. But things never hit in the same way again. In the middle of the club in the early hours of the morning, he looked around and said to himself: "What am I doing? I don't even know who I am. What are all these people doing?"

The highs had peaked, and the comedowns became darker than before. Emptiness characterized his lifestyle, yet he still didn't want to give his life to God because he knew it would mean giving up control.

While a spiritual longing had now kicked in, it was in fact another year until Lewis finally came to his senses and surrendered his life to Jesus. Giles still journeyed side by side with him in this period, and the unspoken agreement between them both was that any decision to follow Jesus had to come from Lewis. Lewis described it to me like God let him live his own way in that time because even God was saying that he had to make the choice for himself.

You can't walk with Jesus *for* others. You can only lead others *to* Jesus. It is their faith, not yours.

Perhaps this is why when he finally surrendered his life, Lewis became such an outspoken, passionate advocate for Christ. He now supports hundreds of young people and is using a newfound gift of poetry to connect people to God. Life has never been the same.

Lewis's story is yet another reminder that some births take time. But if this is so often the case, then why do we prefer stories about sudden transformations over gradual revelations?

Every Story Has a Beginning

Saul of Tarsus is undoubtedly the historical poster boy for dramatic conversions. He was a man zealously devoted to the destruction of Christians everywhere he went. While traveling on the road to Damascus, he was met with a blinding light, fell off his horse, and became totally transformed by Jesus. Saul became Paul and was never the same man again.

Yet, even sudden conversions have hidden beginnings. Although he may not have been seeking God, God was most definitely seeking him. Saul had a deeply personalized experience that was necessary for his particular situation, and an extreme experience was required to snap him out of his extreme behavior. But this wasn't his only encounter with Jesus. I wonder if his previous experience with Stephen the Martyr (see Acts 7:57–60) still spoke to Saul? He had already seen God working among the community he was busy trying to destroy. While Saul's origin is significant *for* the church, it's not representative of every person's story *in* the church.

Everybody starts their journey with Jesus somewhere. If the result of effective discipleship ends with Christlikeness, then an obvious question to ask is, Where does it actually start? If you ask people how they came to faith in Jesus, you'll hear as many stories as there are people. I've seen rapid turnarounds in people's lives, but they're often the exception rather than the rule. Many become aware of the dawn rather than blinded by the light.

Paul would have fallen off his horse again if someone tried to tell him that everyone would have to come to Christ in the same way that he did. For example, when he went to Mars Hill in Athens and shared about Jesus (see Acts 17), they met him with a mixture of sneers and enquiries. Some of the Athenians asked for more time to talk through what this gospel message meant for them in their cultural context. They needed a process ministry, not a platform one.

The disciples Peter, James, John, and Mary all had unique paths to their spiritual formation and ultimate conversion. A fun theological question to ask yourself is, When did the disciples actually get saved? They often had a bumpy road to revelation, and their understanding of Christ varied, even after they had been with him in the flesh for three years. They needed constant reassurance and answers to endless questions from Jesus about Jesus before they threw themselves all in.

Elsewhere in Acts 18:24–26, we see the example of Apollos who had some understanding of faith from the baptism of John and even passionately spoke about Jesus to lots of people, but he basically didn't know what he was talking about. Priscilla and Aquila, who heard him in the temple, had to invite him to their home and—in Luke's not-so-subtle words—"explain the way of God more adequately." That's a polite way of saying that they stopped him spouting heresy.

I honestly think if some churches could, they would hand out horses for people to fall off because it would look brilliant on social media. So why do we so often expect people to come to Christ in a sudden or exciting way? Why do we so often build our methods around creating the expectation of a highly emotional moment of drama? At best, we don't fully understand the process toward conversion. At worst, we favor short-term success rather than long-term transformation because of our own egos. Drama makes us look better.

Every Big Story Has Little Chapters

Back in the 1970s, researcher James Engel became fascinated by the diminishing effectiveness of church outreach, including the long-term impact of the popular large-scale evangelistic events at the time. They reported thousands of people converting night after night, raising their hands, running down to the altar, and filling in response cards. The community was expected to balloon as a result, yet even just a short time later, the number of people who were actually added to the local church was negligible.

These events were making countless converts but rarely making disciples. Despite this evidence, an increasing amount of effort seemed to go into engineering platform experiences that favored sudden moments of conversion. Arguing that we should focus on the process not just the platform, Engel and his colleague Wilbert Norton wrote their seminal book, *What's Gone Wrong with the Harvest?*[1]

Before we go on, I want to share a personal note on this topic of mass outreach because I don't want you to think I'm writing it off completely. A few years back, I was showing my father-in-law, Paul, a coffee table book called *Billy Graham: God's Ambassador* when he flicked through the pages and stopped at an image of Earl's Court Arena in London. The picture was from 1966 at one of the many evangelistic campaigns with which Graham is synonymous. Paul gestured to the grainy photo and said, "I became a Christian because of that meeting."

The story goes that Paul had been invited by a Christian friend to attend a live television relay of the event and ended up giving his life to Christ. The rest is now part of my history. Paul became an incredibly faithful disciple of Jesus and continued his journey, which resulted in him leading a church in Wakefield and his family being saved. So if according to research, the long-term success rates for stadium crusades are somewhere near one thousand-to-one, I have to say I am forever grateful for that *one*. My family would not be who it is without Billy Graham and those like him who were obedient to their calling in their context. It's also worth pointing out that while this is a story of conversion at a big event, it started with a small invite from a friend.

The point made by Engel and Norton was not so much to criticize one particular method but to make us rethink the whole idea of conversion altogether. They developed the world-famous Engel Scale to benchmark the journey someone took from not knowing God through to spiritual maturity over several stages. This idea was revolutionary, not only because it recognized the steps a person had to take after their conversion, but also the ones they made before it.

Here are the numbered stages an average person likely passes through before they decide to follow Christ:[2]

The Engel Scale	
-10	Awareness of the supernatural
-9	No effective knowledge of Christianity
-8	Initial awareness of Christianity
-7	Interest in Christianity
-6	Awareness of basic facts of the gospel
-5	Grasp of implications of the gospel
-4	Positive attitude to the gospel
-3	Awareness of personal need
-2	Challenge and decision to act
-1	Repentance and faith
0	A disciple is born!

When I first heard Lewis tell me his story about how he came to Christ, I could almost picture him moving down the Engel Scale toward Jesus. While there has been some criticism leveled at its linear approach, I still consider the Engel Scale ground-breaking because it reframed evangelism as helping anyone take a step toward Jesus, no matter where they are on their spiritual journey.

Right at the back end, you have someone who may have an awareness of spiritual things but no concept of Christ or Christianity. You would treat this person very differently from the one who already has a working knowledge of the gospel. Discerning where a person is on the scale helps you prayerfully point them toward Christ. A step in the right direction is better than no step at all.

Many have modernized the language of the Engel Scale over the years, with updated versions adding in more stages before or after the point of decision. It's interesting that some of these newer editions fall foul of the desire to "churchify" people after their conversion. But the potency of the original Engel Scale is that it encourages you to focus on influencing the tangible steps people take toward Jesus before they make a fully considered decision to follow Christ.

Every Story Has Another Page

Speaking on the *Vanderbloemen Leadership Podcast*, church strategist Tony Morgan notes how he has shaped his strategic approach to disciple-making based on his own decoding of the steps he first took toward Christ:

> I just kind of went back a number of months ago and started to look at my personal spiritual journey from a point where I wasn't interested or even aware of things related to faith. And then through a series of circumstances, I would argue, I became curious about faith and who Jesus was. And then eventually, I became a believer and then I was discipled, and then I became a disciple maker. And there are different nuances, you may be familiar with the Engel Scale, different nuances of what those steps look like.[3]

From his own journey, Morgan developed a *discipleship pathway*, which is a simplified version of the Engel Scale marking five stages of maturity for any disciple.

- *Stage 1:* Not Interested
- *Stage 2:* Spiritually Curious
- *Stage 3:* Becoming a Believer
- *Stage 4:* Being Discipled
- *Stage 5:* Becoming a Disciple Maker

It is this shift from "Stage 1: Not Interested" to "Stage 2: Spiritually Curious" that I believe is the most neglected focus across the church. We have so many resources, programs, preachers, and platforms dedicated to helping people once they're in the door, and so few strategies, hints, and tips for when they are still at the initial stage of exploration.

In their outreach training from the Baptist Union of Great Britain,[4] the importance of the Engel Scale is raised when it comes to effectiveness on the mission field. Their training starts by asking participants two simple questions to highlight an obvious missed opportunity:

> *Question 1:* Where on the scale are most people in England?
>
> *Answer:* At the lower end of the Engel Scale.
>
> *Question 2:* Where on the scale has our evangelism been directed?
>
> *Answer:* At the higher end of the Engel Scale.

If we don't pay attention to where people are really at, then we will never scratch where people are itching. Some might read this and think the answer is just to make sure you put on an Alpha course at your local church. The Alpha course is a space where people come together to ask the big questions of life. You gather—online or in person—and watch a series of episodes that explore the basics of the Christian faith. There is no doubt that Alpha is an effective tool for evangelism. In fact, a Barna Study found that 93 percent of churches describe it as so. The results of the program are astonishing. Since doing Alpha, 82 percent of non-Christians have described themselves as becoming followers of Jesus![5]

But the important question here is what happens *before* Alpha? What about those who can't sign up for a three-month program or the ones who aren't yet ready to take part in a small group discussion about Jesus because they don't even know his name yet? This is where our sense of individual responsibility to be a disciple-maker has to kick in.

The whole point of any scale, whether there are two steps or ten in it, is that there are clear stages for people to walk through before they come to a point of commitment to Christ, not just work to do afterwards. The ultimate goal of taking more of a process-oriented approach is that it means we can develop a lifestyle that reaches people wherever they are. As one blogger puts it,

> How do I use the Engel Scale? Simple: I use it all the time, with everybody I meet. My goal for every relationship in my life is to encourage each person to trust God with more and more of their own life. If they are only aware of the basic story of Jesus, I want them to understand the fundamentals of the gospel, and to grasp what it means to them. If they're already born again, I work to encourage them to continue moving toward maturity.[6]

This concept is a game changer that radically informs our mission, our methods, and our messages. It redefines our measures for success and opens up the playing field for *all* Christians to be involved in the process of disciple making.

Start where you are. Start where they are. Learn to trust the process of simply helping others take their next tangible step.

REFLECT ═══

Retrace your own spiritual journey and see how it fits into the Engel Scale.

- *How fast did you move through each phase?*
- *Was there ever a time where you were stuck for a while?*
- *How did you become unstuck?*

These are vital reflections that can help you decode your own walk so you can help others.

5

DEVELOPING

For, "Everyone who calls on the name of the Lord will be saved."

Romans 10:13

In the summer of 2008, teenager Sarah Ruscoe wanted to throw a party to celebrate her eighteenth birthday at her parents' twenty-one-bedroom mansion in rural England while they were out of town. On the day of the party, her friend persuaded Pete Tong, a popular BBC Radio 1 DJ, to do a shout-out for the event on the radio. It was a joke that backfired famously. The whole thing snowballed until two thousand people showed up! It took a battalion of police, two angry parents, and a disgruntled bunch of neighbors to get the party to stop. In typical British passive-aggressive style, Sarah's mother, angry about what the DJ did (perhaps as transference instead of dealing with her own daughter's folly), told ABC News, "I'm going to write a stiff letter to ask the BBC to review its policy." We Brits love to write a stiff letter when things don't go our way!

This story reminds us about the power of an invitation. Both evangelism and discipleship are about making invitations for people to take another step toward Jesus depending on their stage on the journey. When it feels like we are stagnant, stuck, or have reached a dead end in our pursuit of God's mission, maybe it's because we've stopped inviting people to make progress.

It would be easy to criticize concepts like the Engel Scale by saying they're too linear. We know that the process of growth and change is often all over the place. It can feel as if you're going round in circles, taking one step forward and two steps back. But we need to remember that the direction of travel is always more important than the pace of the journey.

It's helpful to name and identify the space where people can explore Jesus before they even enter the threshold of the church and a counterculture that's often quite foreign to them. The word *pre-discipleship* can be defined as helping people take small steps toward Christ *before* they take big steps with him.

Thinking about the term "pre-discipleship" encourages us to focus on preparing people *before* their moment of decision just as much as we do *after* it. It's about asking, How do we help prepare the way for people to move from being not interested to becoming spiritually curious?

Author Kai Mark was one of the first I heard talking about pre-discipleship, and in his book by the same name, he points to its origins amongst the first-century disciples:

> It is evident that the pre-discipleship process was practiced in the New Testament and in the early church before baptism. The catechumenate gave evidence that converts to Christianity had systematic teaching before they could be baptized. This was another confirmation of the existence of a pre-discipleship process in the early church.[1]

"Cata-what-now?" I hear you say. Well, the word *catechumenate* basically refers to any group of people who receive instruction in the Christian faith in order to prepare themselves to be baptized. Between about AD 100 and 300, seekers who wanted to become part of the church had to undergo a lengthy induction process. They had to show their commitment to a lifestyle of following Christ. This was all before they could formally become part of the church community.

The irony is that two thousand years ago, because of the focus on disciple-making, people were almost discouraged from joining the church unless they were serious about it. Whereas nowadays we're often so wrapped up in improving our church attendance levels, we can neglect prioritizing disciple-making!

Not only was pre-discipleship supposedly a common practice in the early church, but there are multiple biblical metaphors that point to the idea that there is a lead-up to a person's moment of conversion. Here are three of them.

Picture 1: Like Being Born

Jesus replied, "Very truly I tell you, no one can see the king-dom of God unless they are born again."

"How can someone be born when they are old?" Nicodemus asked. "Surely they cannot enter a second time into their mother's womb to be born!" (John 3:3–4)

Nicodemus was a man who had spent his whole life being shaped by religious tradition, righteous acts, and so-called *right* ways of thinking. Yet when he came to Christ, he realized none of that mattered if he wasn't willing to let Jesus change him from the inside out. He was being actively discipled in the wrong direction and needed a rebirth.

What I love about the image of new birth is that it perfectly illustrates the paradox that something can be both gradual and sudden at the same time. During early pregnancy, things seem to move at a micro pace. Outwardly, nothing seems to happen, yet there are miracles that go on inside the mother's womb. The groundwork for the digestive system, lungs, heart, brain, nervous system, and even tooth enamel are being slowly formed, layer by layer, within the first four to five weeks of unseen growth.

Before the birth of our firstborn, Nyah, my wife felt the early pains of pre-labor a few days after her due date. Not understanding what full labor really felt like, we were convinced she was ready to pop and so we went to the hospital. It turned out we were a little too keen. As we entered the elevator to go up to the maternity ward, we were greeted with a taste of what was to come.

A woman was being wheeled on a trolley to the ward ahead of us, looking like she had just returned from the throngs of a great battle. She was drenched in sweat and screaming at the top of her lungs. With every contraction, her partner looked on as helpless as the child that was about to be born.

"Oh, *that's* what real labor looks like!" we said to each other with a hint of fear. It was a far cry from the minor pangs of pre-labor. Process takes patience.

They sent us away from the hospital after a quick check-up. Having no car of our own, we thought our best bet was to camp out at my parents' house, which was near the hospital, until things really got going. I have vivid memories of my dad sitting happily in the living room reading the paper while my wife paced back and forth, groaning, in the open-plan dining room!

After what seemed like ages, we finally returned to the maternity ward and were declared officially in labor. I gave myself a medal and a pat on the back, then progress escalated quickly. My wife's waters broke just at the moment the nurses went for a quick cup of tea! After our daughter was born, the pain of labor soon turned to tears of joy.

"What's wrong with her lungs?" I asked the nurse as I held my little girl for the first time and watched as she breathed erratically.

"Her lungs are fine," she replied with a smile on her face. "She's just never used them before."

Now that she's an adult herself, I can confirm and testify that Nyah's lungs really are fine.

Pregnancy and birth are two distinctly different phases, but they are intrinsically connected. The former is a period of transition that prepares you physically, mentally, and emotionally for the dramatic change that is to come. There is a slow process and then a sudden moment. There is perhaps no greater illustration of pre-discipleship than this. Like the pregnancy stage, each person has their own journey of development before they come to Christ. Then there is the moment of decision to follow Christ, which is like the birth itself. Based on this analogy, it would be inconceivable to consider newborn babies outside of the connection to pregnancy. Birthing doesn't happen in isolation. And just as a newborn baby needs support, love, and care in order to grow, so the process of incubation and growing to spiritual maturity begins after conversion. Each stage needs a different type of care and attention, but each one is vital.

Picture 2: Like Building a Tower

"Suppose one of you wants to build a tower. Won't you first sit down and estimate the cost to see if you have enough money to complete it? For if you lay the foundation and are not able to finish it, everyone who sees it will ridicule you, saying, 'This person began to build and wasn't able to finish.'"
(Luke 14:28–30)

At more than twenty-seven hundred feet, the Burj Khalifa in Dubai is the world's tallest building. Its iconic image was thrust into popular culture by Tom Cruise, who spent a good portion of the fourth *Mission Impossible* film hanging off it. The tower stands high over a city that is renowned, not just for its incredible examples of architecture, but also for being a graveyard of failed architectural schemes. The area is full of half-completed projects and plans that never quite got off the ground. There are many ideas commissioned by overambitious entrepreneurs with too much time and money on their hands that never saw the light of day.

Have you heard about the visionary who wanted to create thirty-two black-and-white skyscrapers in the shape of a complete chess set and call it International Chess City? Checkmate. Sadly, there weren't enough chess lovers for this genius idea to catch on. And of course, there are the World Islands, a set of floating, man-made islands shaped like every country on earth. Someone cunningly made it without considering the fact that nobody actually wanted it. I'm sure that somewhere in a half-finished building in Dubai, there's a secret club that meets to discuss their next hair-brained projects and half-baked ideas.

Jesus likens starting the discipleship journey to a builder who must make a sober assessment before they begin. He is proactively trying to discourage people from deciding to follow him if they're not willing to count the cost. It's almost as if Jesus is saying, "Sit back for a minute and plan for your future. Lay out two blueprints on the table. One has your life with me in the center, and the other has life without me. Now be very sure what you want to build with your life."

The speed of this sober assessment will inevitably vary from person to person. For some, they could make this decision in a moment. Others will really need to think it through. Although we don't want anyone to become stuck at this stage, it certainly can't be skipped without risking serious complications down the line. In many respects, we could argue that the depth to which someone sees the reality of the treasure of Christ will determine how much they'll give up to follow him.

For those of us who have the privilege of pointing people to follow Jesus, we must ensure there is space for a noncoercive decision-making process that begins with full consent. Jesus never manipulated anyone into following him.

Picture 3: Like Planting Seed in the Soil

"But the seed falling on good soil refers to someone who hears the word and understands it. This is the one who produces a crop, yielding a hundred, sixty or thirty times what was sown." (Matt. 13:23)

When Jesus taught the parable of the sower, he was teaching his disciples that not everyone would be in the same place when they heard the message of truth. Even though the seed of the Word is always potent, the conditions in which it is planted will affect the level of fruitfulness.

The condition of our heart affects our response to the Word of God. Therefore, the very early stages of pre-discipleship are vital as we help break up the fallow ground, getting it ready for God to speak. Rather than accepting a one-in-four success ratio as a fait accompli, what if Jesus is giving us a kind of insight into how we can work with people to prepare the soil?

A person might feel far from God because they don't *know* (ignorance about Jesus) or they don't *care* (apathy toward Christ) or a combination of both. This paradigm can be applied to the parable of the sower and the seed.

- "I don't know, and I don't care" (the hard heart).
- "I do care, but I don't know" (the shallow heart).
- "I do know, but I don't care" (the crowded heart).

Each type of person requires a different pre-discipleship approach. Once we prayerfully discern where a person is on their journey, we can then take practical steps to help them where they're at.

"I don't know, and I don't care." For the hard-hearted, we must become prayer warriors. It's interesting that Jesus mentions the "evil one" only for this type of person, which shows that there may be an unhealthy spiritual influence that can be broken only through prayer. So many people end up with truth snatched from under their nose because of a calloused heart. This may be because of their own stubbornness, or it may be because of pain caused by others. Spiritual hardness is a difficult problem to solve by earthly means. To walk side by side with them, we have to pray.

"I do care, but I don't know." For the shallow-hearted, we must become companions. They need to put down roots quickly before it's too late. We have to take the window of opportunity to walk alongside pre-disciples when they become curious. Some people like the idea of finding faith, but they don't know what to do next. Too often, we just assume that new people will figure it out for themselves, but we need to help them learn the skills to sustain their enthusiasm so that it doesn't wane at the first sign of trouble. We can't leave anyone to their own devices. To walk side by side with them, we have to befriend them.

"I do know, but I don't care." For the crowded heart, we must become guides. They may have seen something of the truth, but it still remains one option among many. Can we help them filter

out what really matters amid the allure of all that glitters? We need them to focus on who Jesus is so that they can overcome the worries of life and the distractions of culture. We do this by building relationships, asking the right questions, and helping people constantly reorientate their compass toward truth. To walk alongside them, we have to guide.

Whether we act as a prayer warrior, a companion, or a guide for people, we're breaking up the fallow ground over time, with a goal to move others to the point of *"I do care, and I do know."* This is the beginning of the path to fruitfulness and multiplication.

Each of these metaphors—the birth, the tower, and the soil—requires a process but are each seeded with the promise of growth.

REFLECT ═══

Consider the parable of the soil in relation to one or two of the people you're walking with right now.

- *Into which category would you say they fall?*

  > *"I don't know, and I don't care."*

  > *"I do care, but I don't know."*

  > *"I do know, but I don't care."*

- *What might the next step look like for them?*

6

Drawing

*"And I, when I am lifted up from the earth,
will draw all people to myself."*

John 12:32

As a nineteen-year-old church youth leader in Cardiff, Wales, I found that my small but passionate group of teenagers was desperate to see more young people encounter Jesus. As youth leaders, we decided the best way to achieve this was to put on a huge outreach event and do it for the young people rather than equip them to reach out themselves! So, we committed loads of time, energy, and effort into planning what we thought would be a world-changing event for the thousands who would turn up just because we invited them.

Why do we always default to going big or going home?

The advertising had gone far and wide across the entire church community, and the day of the big event finally arrived. As the evening began, we realized that the numbers were going to be much less than expected. In fact, they were almost nonexistent. Suddenly the four-hundred-seater auditorium felt twice as big as usual! There was barely a new face in the house. In fact, there was barely a face in the house. Already feeling a sense of disappointment kick in, we went ahead with the program anyway and hoped it would bless the small group of young people who had gathered.

Then, just before we introduced the first item on our agenda, the most unexpected thing happened.

Smash! Bang! Thud.

There was a loud crash and seemingly out of nowhere, a soccer ball smashed through one of the church hall windows, landing near the stage. A few seconds later, there was a banging at the rear fire doors, and we let a sheepish-looking young lad in a tracksuit into the hall looking like he was about to face a firing squad. He was so unassuming and apologetic that you couldn't stay mad at him for very long. He picked up his ball, brushed off the glass, and looked around at the stage, the band, and the tiny audience.

"What's going on here?" he curiously asked once he knew he would not be reported to the police.

We explained it was a Christian event for young people with music, performances, and stories. Amazingly, he asked, "Can I stay around?" Turns out this young man, let's call him Callum, was from the Flaxland estate that lay behind the church building and had been kicking a ball around by himself. He then sat with us through the next hour of our best efforts to execute an engaging extravaganza to a near empty room. At the end of the evening, we chatted with Callum further and discovered that he was cheeky, a little rogue, and instantly likable.

"What's happening next week?" he asked, just before leaving through the same back door he entered earlier that night.

No one had really thought that through.

"Erm . . . We'll be back here again," one of us said.

"Cool, I'll see you then," he replied. "And I'll bring my mates."

That "failed" youth outreach event triggered the biggest growth our youth group had seen in a long time. Something drew Callum toward belonging, and it turns out later this curiosity would lead to him following Jesus. It was either completely by coincidence or completely by God. Either way, we're not sure we had anything to do with it.

First Callum broke our window, and then he broke our program. After that, we had to change everything about the strategy for our youth group. The old "worship-and-word" model wasn't working, and we ended up starting a café for young people called

"React." It was a mixture of games, fun, short talks, and lots of laughter and relationship building. Callum became one of the young men we walked alongside for a season as we introduced him to Jesus, along with many of his friends.

The day that window broke in the church building, I felt a few illusions about how God works also shatter. Never in a million years could we have orchestrated a ball to crash through a window on exactly the right night at exactly the right time. We concluded that God must have been at work drawing Callum to himself and using us despite ourselves. And this is the point, isn't it? Drawing people to Christ is already happening.

We don't journey toward God unless God first journeys toward us.

The Draw to Something Deeper

Countless people like Callum are desperately looking for answers in life. Yet there is a generation emerging that increasingly feels like the church has no place in satisfying their deep level of spiritual curiosity. The growing gap between the church and the world seems to be widening by the day. This is a chasm that one side or the other must cross.

Through a school-based charity called Grace Foundation, I have been working for over a decade with young people who have no church background. This is where the gap feels widest to me. The COVID-19 pandemic meant not only lost learning for students but also a myriad of issues, including intense academic pressure, feelings of loneliness, peer issues, poor well-being, mental health challenges, and financial hardship in families. Without the work of the Grace Foundation Team, even considering any kind of Christian perspective as a solution to these issues would probably be the last thing a young person would choose to do.

Today, the thousands of young people we engage with daily are full of questions about life; they are passionate, brilliant, and fun. But they are also under more pressure than ever, full of anxiety and confusion, and desperately seeking a sense of identity and purpose. Young people follow a digital algorithm that knows them better than most of the adults in their life. If you were to mention that Jesus wanted to be the savior of their souls, they would likely look at you with slightly glazed eyes before returning to scrolling on their phone. This is not because they aren't spiritual, but because their only reference point to the word *Jesus* is likely a meme they have seen on the internet.

Even though deep down, I know many of them long to hear some sort of good news, I have a niggling concern that faith is not on their radar as the answer. This is natural because it's no longer widely considered by the society around them. For example, Pew Research did a survey in multiple countries to determine what gives people meaning in their life.[1] Out of a list of seventeen options for what gives them a sense of purpose, faith did not appear in the top ten of the countries except for the United States. Even there, they listed faith fifth behind family, friends, material well-being, and occupation. Most countries consider their hobbies as more of a source of hope than their faith. We now live in a world where golf comes before God!

Yet there is something encouraging bubbling beneath the surface of this next generation. Barna's research shows that young Millennial non-Christians talk about spiritual matters a lot more than older adults. They are also twice as likely to express a personal interest in Christianity as other generations.[2] And their preferred means of exploring Christianity is not via a tract, video, small group, or podcast. It is in fact by talking one on one with someone who is a Christian. If that first phase of the Engel Scale is about moving people from being uninterested to becoming spiritually curious, then perhaps there is hope for us yet.

The Draw to Come and See

In John 1:38–39 when Jesus first met some of John the Baptist's friends, they were curious about who he was and wanted to know more. Noticing that they were intentionally hanging around and clearly looking for engagement, Jesus asked them a killer question and then gave them a brilliant next step:

> Turning around, Jesus saw them following and asked, "What do you want?"
>
> They said, "Rabbi" (which means "Teacher"), "where are you staying?"
>
> "Come," he replied, "and you will see."

This phrase "come and see" is a powerful invitation that taps into the heart of the spiritually curious. It's a shame that some churches struggle to make the same invitation because they don't value the exploration stage enough. There are others, however, who grasp just how vital this is.

A few years ago, I had the privilege of seeing what harnessing a culture of curiosity might look like in action through attending a youth conference called "Fusiondary" in the Czech Republic. Believe it or not, it was an international gathering of youth rock and gospel choirs led by a Christian ministry called Josiah Venture.

Over nine hundred young people, many with very little church background, came together from nine countries to dance, play music, and sing in choirs together. What was unique was not just their ability to cater to people from diverse nations but also to cater to young people who were at wildly different points on their own journeys of faith. The room was full of people who were a mix of *I-don't-know* and *I-don't-care* hearts and every combination of the soil parable in between.

While singing was the core activity, the spiritual spin-offs were tangible. The process formed strong relationships between churches and young people. Some of the music was faith based but never cringy, which led to plenty of opportunities for discussion. The laughter level was at least one hundred decibels. The speakers on the stage focused on interviews and storytelling, not preaching. Optional seminars were available with topics from practical video making to learning how to pray. Everyone was valued and included, no matter what stage of the spiritual journey they were on. You could literally see people sliding down the Engel Scale before your very eyes!

It's interesting how often you can see the theology of a ministry in action before you read about it on their website. This was so clear with Josiah Venture. First, they make music, and then they make disciples. Their level of commitment to helping people take small steps toward Jesus was exemplary. I found out later that they root their strategy in what they call the "five challenges of Christ." This quote from their teaching explains:

> In the Gospels, we see this process of disciple making modeled in the way Christ challenged his followers from their initial positions of unbelief to a point of spiritual maturity and fruitfulness. The disciple making process can be summed up in five basic challenges from the ministry of Christ. "Come and see" (to expose), "repent and believe" (to evangelize), "follow me" (to build), "I will make you fishers of men" (to equip), and "I am sending you" (to send).[3]

It is this call to "come and see" that was so clear in the Czech Republic gathering. Giving room to "come and see" is fundamental to the spiritual formation of those who don't yet know Christ. Too often, we try to skip through this stage and get people to sign on the dotted line rather than help them respond to the invitation to *come and see.* This isn't just about how we structure our corporate outreach gatherings; it's also about how we personally provide space to allow others to express their own sense of curiosity.

The Draw to Be Curious

Ever since we heard that a cat died because of it, we tend to see the idea of being curious as risky. On the surface, we may be encouraged by the traditional education establishment to be open to new ideas and experiences; but subliminally, we're expected not to rock the boat or question anything. And in some ways, there is a danger that our inquisitiveness can lead us down the wrong path or cause us to deconstruct ourselves to where there's nothing left to build back up with. Yet to be incurious is even more dangerous. It's far costlier to become disinterested, disengaged, and indifferent.

In a collection of essays, *Radical Hope: Letters of Love and Dissent in Dangerous Times*, writer Celeste Ng recalls speaking to her son about the importance of why curiosity is such a key value for life:

> Being curious is admitting that you don't know, but also that you want to know. That what you don't know is worth knowing. That people you don't know are worth knowing, that they have something to teach you. That learning about them—that encountering new ideas—doesn't threaten you, it enriches you. That what you haven't experienced is worth experiencing. That you approach the world as a trove of things to take in, rather than things you frantically, fearfully wall out.[4]

Albert Einstein famously encouraged people to "never lose a holy curiosity." This means to approach life with a sense of inquisitiveness rooted in awe and wonder. There are two ways we can put this into practice in our side-by-side journeys with others.

First, we need to learn to develop a *holy curiosity* about those with whom we are walking side-by-side. This starts with us letting go of the assumptions that we already know all there is to know about them. This is not about being invasive or intrusive, but about being genuinely concerned for others. If we don't ask questions, then we'll learn nothing new. In fact, if we spend less time jumping to conclusions and more time listening, then it's much more likely that those with whom we're walking will respond in the same way to us.

Second, we need to create a kind of nonjudgmental atmosphere in our relationships where *holy curiosity* can be expressed without us becoming overexcited or going over the top. We tend to want to rush people through this exploration stage, but this is the space where important foundations are being laid behind the scenes. If we can just resist the temptation to be judgmental and critical of others when their journey or questioning doesn't seem to go according to our expectations, it can open up opportunities for awe and wonder.

We are often wise not to disturb the chrysalis lest the butterfly fail to emerge.

While we don't need to be threatened by exploration, we do need to be prepared for it. Readiness comes when we know where to direct people to their *next step* and not leave them wandering. It's about being present to answer questions and signpost to the way, the truth, and the life. It's about being continually patient with the process, always praying that the Holy Spirit will bring the breakthrough, and trusting the outcome to God.

Darin and Joy Stevens, founders of Start to Stir, a missional training organization, call this delicate process of cultivating curiosity the art of "stirring souls." They encourage people to look inward rather than outward if those people want to connect with their Creator in a world where God seems largely irrelevant:

> Over the past twenty years of working with youth in a post-Christian context, we have found that one of the most effective starting points to overcome this "relevancy barrier" to the gospel and arouse spiritual curiosity is by helping people to experience the reality that, as humans, we have a soul. Rather than attempting to use logic to convince individuals there is a God who is "out there," we can rely on what God has already placed "in there" to stimulate curiosity and then to point to longings that cannot be satisfied by the limits of self or the confines of this present life.[5]

Pointing to the evidence of our human soul and the longings of the human heart can begin to stir a desire for something more.

There is an entrepreneurial collective of writers, thinkers, and producers at the Something More Creative Agency who declare that their mission is to "show people Jesus." They produce articles, podcasts, clothing, devotionals, print publications, trips, and events that invite people to discover Christ, relevantly. Whether in a magazine or on a T-shirt, hoodie, or tote bag, they invite consumers to reflect on simple statements such as, "There is something more."

By presenting "something more" as a concept, this will hopefully prompt people to ask questions or give the wearer a boost of courage to talk about what "something more" looks like in their everyday life. These hooks act as catalysts for meaning, identity, and truth. We don't need to feel pressure to give anyone everything on a plate in one go. Let people go digging for themselves. You don't have to wear a hoodie with a slogan to be a signpost. In fact, later in the book we'll be exploring many practical ways we can do this. But for now, we see that our role is to live a life that gives people a safe space to express their holy curiosity.

In the meantime, a question probably worth being curious about is this: "Will others find *something more* through me?"

REFLECT ════════════════════════════════════

- *What do you think are the signs that someone in your life is becoming more curious about spirituality, faith, or God?*

- *What might you do to prepare for this?*

- *How are you helping or hindering curiosity by the way you live your life?*

7

STUMBLING

*"Peace I leave with you; my peace I give you. I do
not give to you as the world gives. Do not let your
hearts be troubled and do not be afraid."*

John 14:27

The documentary *Free Solo*, a portrait of climber Alex Honnold,
is almost too incredible to believe, but it's definitely real. The
film follows Honnold as he prepares to climb the face of the
three-thousand-foot El Capitan in Yosemite National Park without a rope. There was literally no safety net and no going back.
The film crew would either see him climb to victory or fall to
his death.

I first watched this intense documentary on a plane on my
way to California, and I was so excited because I knew in a few
short days I would actually get to see "El Cap" in Yosemite and
this sheer rock face, also known as the Dawn Wall, for myself.
Being the adventurer that I am, I was inspired to have a go at
climbing while I was there. So after watching the movie, reading
a short blog, and declaring myself an expert, when we finally
got to the breathtakingly beautiful Yosemite, I knew my moment
had come.

Amid the rocky landscape, I saw a six-foot smooth boulder
and thought I would start my practice ascent. Sadly, even after
the inspiration of watching Alex Honnold scale a mountain, I
failed to even get my foot to grip on a small rock. Apparently
watching someone on television do it doesn't count as training

for yourself! Alex may have had no rope, but I had no hope! I couldn't help but be impressed with my utter failure to get just over two feet off the ground. It's incredible how quickly fear kicks in at even the lowest of heights. My feet could not get a grip, and neither could my mind.

I discovered that just because we see it doesn't mean we can do it. If we don't have the same training, skill base, or background, there's little hope of us being able to step up to the plate. So what hope have we got, then, for imitating Christ in how he makes disciples? We cannot do this with our own strength. We cannot rely on natural talent.

Without Jesus, we can't get even a foot off the ground.

There are so many barriers and stumbling blocks that Christians must overcome to help people kick-start their journey with Jesus. You can call them mental blockages or misunderstandings, but they are usually just expressions of fear.

There has been some really interesting recent research by the Barna Group that digs into why many Christians struggle with disciple-making.[1] Much of it is based on the fact that we don't see ourselves as qualified or equipped to do so. In some ways, we see the professional preachers and pastors as a spiritual equivalent of a free-solo climber and think, "I could never do that." If discipleship and evangelism are that technical or difficult to outwork, then we can be forgiven for avoiding it altogether and thinking that it's someone else's job.

Our excuses to stay on the ground fall into three major categories: being too busy, feeling too ill equipped, and simply being downright scared.

Excuse 1: I'm Too Busy

In a modern world where we don't even have time to read *The Ruthless Elimination of Hurry*, we often struggle to fit Jesus' commission into our stressful schedules. Christians struggle to find time to connect deeply with one another let alone those outside the church. It's not just that we watch movies or TV shows, scroll on social media, or get wrapped up in entertaining pastimes. Nor is it that we're all stressed out with the pressures of work, family, and trying to juggle a thousand responsibilities at once. I think one of the biggest challenges for Christians is how much time we spend wrapped up in church activities that don't move the goalposts of discipleship forward.

We can literally be too busy *doing* church to *be* the church.

I will never forget one of the most cutting comments I've ever received about my faith journey, which came from a housemate at university: "I wouldn't ever become a Christian because I never want to become as busy as you." My proactive involvement in so many church programs (some of which were ironically about reaching out to others) put her off ever engaging with a life following Jesus. It prompted a reassessment.

It's said that on average we each get about four thousand weeks to live. This is a stark reminder to invest what time we have in things that really matter. The question for us is what will we do with the limited resource of time that we have?

- *Mission has to be a matter of priority.* It's so easy to blame external circumstances for our lack of time, although most of us seem to find space for the things we really want to do.

- *Mission is a matter of perspective.* If discipleship is life done side by side with others, then it can be outworked alongside other things we need to achieve.

This is not an excuse to become unintentional, but an invitation to rethink how we see mission altogether. Perhaps it's not always about who I reach out to, but who is already reaching out to me. We just need to slow down enough to pay attention.

Jesus did big, amazing things in his ministry where he reached crowds of people. But at the heart of it, he always stopped for "the one." No matter how big his crowd became, he always thought of "the one."

- *Peter was one:* an insignificant young fisherman in a boat who meets Jesus and ends up being one of the most significant players in the early church.

- *Zacchaeus was one:* a corrupt tax collector who meets Jesus and ends up ushering in a new way of doing kingdom business.

- *Mary Magdalene was one:* a broken woman who meets Jesus and ends up being the most famous worshiper in history.

Heidi Baker is the CEO of Iris Global, a Christian humanitarian organization that has made an impact all over the world. Baker integrates the idea of *stopping for the one* as a core part of the organization's vision. She defines ministry as "simply loving the person in front of you. It's about stopping for the one and being the very fragrance of Jesus to a lost and dying world."[2]

Loving the person in front of you can be done on any schedule. I don't care if you work as a salesperson for a car company or as a receptionist for a doctor's surgery. This is something every Christian can do. You don't need special training, and it doesn't require you to be a superhero. You simply need to be brave enough to press pause and see what happens when you focus on "the one."

Excuse 2: I'm Too Ill Equipped

A pervasive lie has crept in via the modern church that you have to be a professional to be a minister or a missionary. This is clear in the language we use around phrases such as "full-time ministry." We end up longing to be on the church stage because that seems to be the place where God uses people in significant ways.

In many churches, to feature on the platform, you have to have a certain skill set that favors confidence and charisma. Looking a certain way is vital, which in many closed circles still means being white and male and wearing ripped jeans! This makes those who don't fit that rigid criteria feel ill equipped for both ministry and mission. A front-row to back-row mentality creeps in. We subconsciously see the platform as the only place where real *ministry* happens. But when church becomes a spectator sport, then Christians expect to have things done for them rather than take personal responsibility. We pay our pastor to do the mission for us, and we become an audience of consumers rather than a family on a mission.

It's not just stages and sages that cause a perspective problem. There are so many stereotypes and caricatures of mission that even when we think of the word, we automatically default to saying, "It's not for me."

- If we see mission as preaching on a stage, then it's only for the gifted.

- If we see mission just as "going out on the streets," then it's only for the extroverted.

- If we see mission as traveling overseas, then it's only for the wealthy.

- If we see mission as reserved for the most knowledgeable, then it's only for those who have been to seminary.

- If we see mission as an activity for the missions department, then it's only for those who have the time to volunteer.

The truth—as David Platt, author of *Radical*, puts it—is more like this:

> Any Christian can do [discipleship]. You don't need to have inordinate skill or unusual abilities to make disciples. You don't need to be a successful pastor or a charismatic leader to make disciples. You don't need to be a great communicator or an innovative thinker to make disciples. That's why Jesus says every Christian must do this.[3]

This gives us hope that we as ordinary people don't have to be "good enough"; we just have to be available. Reaching people is not the responsibility of a professional pastor or a platform performer; it's our shared collective mandate. Everyone gets to play.

Excuse 3: I'm Too Afraid

None of us like to say this excuse out loud because it hits at the heart of our abdication. We're scared of not knowing what to say, how to respond, or how others will respond to us. We're afraid of stepping out of our comfort zone, especially when it comes to sharing our faith with others. The thing about something new is that it's always scary at first. That's why we need to be willing to enter the *stretch zone*; we need to see something greater beyond our fear. Often, we're fearful because we think that to live a missional lifestyle requires us to do some sort of extreme gesture like jump on a plane or shout from the mountain tops.

It's okay to start small. We tend to think that something that seems small is therefore insignificant. But we need to remember that so much of what God does starts in seed form. Opportunities rarely come in ready-made instant packages. In nature, we have the acorn that turns into the oak tree, or the sperm and the egg that form in the womb to a fully grown human. Even in the Gospel stories, we have the baby in a manger who later becomes the rescuer of the world. Discipleship is simply about being brave enough to help someone take one small step closer to Jesus.

There's No Excuse We Can't Overcome

In the last days of Jesus' time on earth, he taught his followers what was coming next when he would no longer be with them.

> "All this I have spoken while still with you. But the Advocate, the Holy Spirit, whom the Father will send in my name, will *teach* you all things and will remind you of everything I have said to you." (John 14:25–26)

The plan was that Christ would send the Holy Spirit to carry on the role of reminding us who we are and what we are here for.

Honestly, I think that Jesus would have done a much better job of all this himself, but he used imperfect people back then, and he still operates that way today. Jesus left us with all the resources and tools we will ever need to overcome our fear and fulfill his commands.

If I said you were going to climb an enormous mountain on your own with no planning, training, or support, then you would probably freak out. But if I said I was going to give you the world's best equipment, a period of extensive training, and famous adventurer Bear Grylls as your guide, you would definitely see it differently. Having Bear Grylls walk you through what needed to happen and then tell you he was coming with you and that he would even bring the backpack would change your entire outlook on any difficult expedition.

The most important lesson we can ever learn is to trust the work of the Holy Spirit in our lives to help us overcome our excuses.

- The Bible describes the Holy Spirit as our teacher; the Spirit is there to walk us through our fears.

- The Bible describes the Holy Spirit as our advocate; the Spirit is there to remind us we are not alone.

- The Bible describes the Holy Spirit as our guide; the Spirit is there to lead us in the right direction.

We have God with us. An experience of the tangible presence of God is so much more than a temporary emotional feeling or the adrenaline we feel in a lively meeting. It's about knowing the joy, peace, and goodness of God that helps us overcome our anxiety. As we wait on God and see things from his perspective, we find our way through fear.

The Holy Spirit has given us everything we need. We have the world's best equipment and heaven's best guide to support us every step of the way. At the end of the day, we all know that fear is, well, scary! This is when we have to come back to the core of what being a disciple is all about: obedience. The more we say yes to God, the more we learn to say no to our excuses.

Ultimately, the antidote to being lost in busyness, having feelings of inadequacy, or being downright afraid is not just to change the way we behave, but to transform our mindset about who we are altogether. Now is the time to understand that we are God's ambassadors.

REFLECT ══

- *Which of the three excuses—too busy, too ill equipped, or too frightened—is holding you back from stepping out on a mission?*

- *How does knowing that you have the Holy Spirit as your teacher, advocate, and guide change your perspective?*

8

SENDING

*We are therefore Christ's ambassadors, as though
God were making his appeal through us. We implore
you on Christ's behalf: Be reconciled to God.*

2 Corinthians 5:20

The 2016 film *Lion* tells the true story of a five-year-old Indian boy, Saroo, who falls asleep alone on a train that takes him thousands of miles across India, far away from his home and family. Saroo must learn to survive alone on the dangerous streets of Kolkata (Calcutta) before ultimately being adopted by a kind Australian couple.

Despite being in a safe and loving home, Saroo cannot reconcile the fact that he doesn't know where he's from, and his life becomes a seemingly endless quest to find his identity and origin. This profoundly affects all of his relationships and his sense of purpose.

Twenty-five years later, Saroo (now played by Dev Patel) sets out to find his lost family and finally returns to his first home. In the story, he spends six long years endlessly searching on what was then new technology, Google Earth, to find the exact location of his home based on his distant memory of roads and rail lines. The sight of Saroo scrolling night after night for who he really was is an analogy that rings true in our souls. Only upon eventually finding his mother again (sorry, I should have said spoiler alert!) in an emotional reunion does he find the peace to move forward.

Saroo's story is, in fact, the story of all of us. We are lost until we know where we came from. Each of us lives with a seemingly endless search for the origin of our identity.

This is a great illustration to use when sharing the gospel. It is not just a story that resonates with those who don't know God but also with those who do. The issue of identity is vital for securing our salvation and for how we change our behavior as a believer toward becoming a missionary.

In his runaway bestseller *Atomic Habits*, writer James Clear asserts that in order to transform our habits, we don't just need to try something different, we must become someone different.

> If you're looking to make a change, then I say stop worrying about results and start worrying about your identity. Become the type of person who can achieve the things you want to achieve. Build identity-based habits now. The results can come later.[1]

For example, if you want to lose weight, become the type of person who does five gym sessions a week. Seeing yourself as a gym person shapes your activities.

An *identity-based habit* is based on the idea that "to change your behavior for good, you need to start believing new things about yourself." Or another way to put it, this is about "who goals" not "do goals." In his Atomic Habits principles, Clear suggests,

> Every action you take is a vote for the type of person you wish to become. No single instance will transform your beliefs, but as the votes build up, so does the evidence of your identity. This is why habits are crucial. They cast repeated votes for being a type of person.[2]

The fundamental difference between the self-help mantra "decide the type of person you want to be" and our own biblical starting point is that we as Christians begin with "accept the person God has made us to be." We are not the creators of our identity but rather the responders to who God created us to be.

Our view of our own identity shapes what we say and do. Therefore, God's identity for us becomes the driver of the activity that comes through us. This identity-driven behavior is clearly seen in the way Jesus operated. The one who went after lost sheep and defended the oppressed is also the one who shows us what life poured out for other people looks like. Why? Because he knew he was on a mission from God. He knew he was *sent*.

Sent by God

There are at least four passages in the Gospel of John where Jesus, knowing he was the Son of God, described himself as being *sent from God*. This "sentness" was evidently a powerful driver for his identity and purpose. Jesus was:

- Secure in God's hands.

- Engaged in God's plans.

- Nourished by God's will.

- Trusting of God's heart.

Jesus was secure in God's hands. Being sent was a sign that Jesus knew his Father defined his identity. He wasn't searching, striving, or scrolling for another source of security other than who he already was. He knew he was equipped because he was God's Son: "I know him because I am from him and he sent me" (John 7:29).

Jesus was engaged in God's plans. He knew his purpose on earth. He didn't get delayed or distracted from living daily in line with his Father's mission. It was not about him. Jesus did not allow busyness to stop him from operating out of who he was: "For I have come down from heaven not to do my will but to do the will of him who sent me" (John 6:38).

Jesus was nourished by God's will. It was completely fulfilling for Jesus to do what he was sent to do. In outworking what God had given him to do on earth, Jesus knew the impact it would have in heaven. So often we are nourished by the adrenaline of a project, the temporary hit of human affirmation, or the chance to prove ourselves. Yet Christ somehow did not find his significance in the work itself but in the One who *sent* him to do it. This is an incredible character attribute we could all learn from. "My food . . . is to do the will of him who *sent* me and to finish his work" (John 4:34).

Jesus was trusting of God's heart. Christ lived a focused life. He did only what he saw his Father doing. The anchor of his life was a faith, hope, and love found in his connection to the Father before his mission in the world. This was a relationship rooted in trust. In Jesus' words as recorded in John 8:29, "The one who *sent* me is with me; he has not left me alone, for I always do what pleases him."

These are compelling thoughts on the nature of Christ. Yet, it is not just Jesus who was sent by God. So are we.

Sent from God

In 2 Corinthians 5:20, Paul describes us as "ambassadors for Christ," which is a mind-blowing concept when you consider it in the context of our identity. An ambassador is "an important official who works in a foreign country representing his or her own country there."[3] They are sent on behalf of another place, deployed on assignment, to let people know about their homeland's intentions, ideas, resources, and messages.

American pastor Jay Pike describes the potency of this analogy in relation to our role as disciples like this: "As an ambassador, we are always representing another culture, we operate out of another value system, we answer to another authority, and we function with another power."[4] Ambassadors approach everything with a different perspective because, much like those from the popular *Undercover Millionaire* TV show, they have access to untapped resources not usually present in the places to which they are sent. This gives them a unique ability to bring about lasting change.

Yet being so metaphorically and spiritually *far from home* is often disorientating and hard. We are homesick for a heaven we have never seen. We desperately miss a king we have never stood before in person. That's why it's important to know what our assignment is when we find ourselves in an unknown place. If we embrace our identity as ambassadors, it changes the way we see ourselves. It helps us to understand the world we are entering and our role in it.

If you're not born in the United Kingdom and want to gain British citizenship, part of what you have to do is pass the Life in the UK Test, which is a set of questions designed to prove your knowledge of British culture and our way of life. As a foreign friend of mine was about to take it, I thought I would try out the test online, especially since the pass rate was a mere 75 percent.

I was fine with starter questions like, "What is the currency of the UK?"

Pretty soon, though, I was in trouble. I may have eaten Yorkshire pudding from the womb, carried a picture of the late great Queen Elizabeth II in my wallet, and even know the words to at least two and a half Beatles songs; but after taking that test, I had some big questions about my own Britishness! Who knows what laws they formed during the swinging sixties? What on earth did Emmeline Pankhurst do for women's rights? (*Who* is Emmeline Pankhurst?)

I only just passed.

Turns out you have to know who you are and where you are from to represent your homeland well. Thankfully, you don't need to attend a program or study for a qualification to become an ambassador. You already are one in Christ.

Sent for God

Being an ambassador has a profound effect on the "who goals" that we set for ourselves. If I see myself as a firefighter, I will take responsibility for running into the burning building, not away from it. In the same way, if I see myself as an ambassador, I will make sure I don't abdicate the role God has given me to live, speak, and act on behalf of Christ. Our sense of identity drives our sense of personal responsibility. By claiming our role as ambassadors, we recognize that:

- We are representatives of a different king.

- We are bridge builders to a different culture.

- We are inviting people to a different way of living.

This idea of being an ambassador wherever we go is fundamental to the concept of walking with others. We can all help others take their first steps toward Christ before they become part of his community. As ambassadors, we invite others to:

- Think differently.

- Try something new.

- Find out more.

As representatives of God, we can learn how to be sensitive to God's Spirit, to harness the power of prayer, and to discern the *next steps* that could move people along their unique journey. Adopting a process-oriented approach to mission or evangelism will help us develop a lifestyle that reaches people wherever they are, at whatever stage they are at. We can start to trust God with the process and let Jesus deal with the outcome.

As ambassadors, we are called to be signposts that direct travelers to their next step on the road toward following Christ. Thankfully, God has not sent us out in isolation to do this signposting, as if we were abandoned emissaries to a forgotten land. We are called to do this together.

There is an unexpectedly powerful scene in one of my wife's favorite family movies *Cheaper by the Dozen* starring Steve Martin. This is a film about Tom and Kate Baker who live in a big house with twelve children. That's one enormous family, and it may be the reason my wife likes it so much. In fact, for years I refused to watch it in case she was trying to use it as a training video!

At one point in the movie, they are facing the pressures of daily life in the house, and after several arguments, disagreements, and selfish moves by different family members, everybody goes underground to find their own space and sulk. The dad is ready to sleep on the couch again, and the kids aren't speaking to one another. The atmosphere is sour, introspective, and toxic. That is until the mother finds a note from one of the youngest children, Mark, saying he had run away because it all had become too much. With two words, the whole household changes: "Mark's gone!"

Instantly, the mood shifts. Petty squabbles are dealt with in seconds, a search party is formed, and a united household goes out to seek the one who has been lost. This is a prodding reminder of what really matters and a powerful picture for the church.

Amid the frustrations we face with those we sometimes take for granted, it's amazing how quickly we forget the small stuff when we rediscover that we are part of a bigger picture. Knowing we are sent means that we can no longer afford to be self-centered. We are God's ambassadors. Together, we are that family on a mission.

REFLECT ══

What goals would you set for yourself if you really understood that you are an ambassador sent by God?

PART TWO

PARALLEL WITH PEOPLE

In this second section of the book, we focus on *how* to start walking alongside others on their journey to Christ. You can start reaching people through a lifestyle of intentional conversations, creativity, care, and connection. In thinking about being *parallel with people,* we will learn that:

✓ Every preparation has a pattern.

✓ Every culture has a context.

✓ Every conversation is a catalyst.

✓ Every believer can be a beholder.

✓ Every creative person is a change-maker.

✓ Every teacher is a trainer.

✓ Every community can care like Christ.

9

PREPARING

But in your hearts revere Christ as Lord. Always be prepared to give an answer to everyone who asks you to give the reason for the hope that you have. But do this with gentleness and respect.

1 Peter 3:15

On a fateful night in 1966, Barbra Streisand, the beloved queen of divas, was performing in Central Park when suddenly she forgot the lyrics to one of her songs. The feeling of being tongue-tied, vulnerable, and so exposed in front of a live audience led her to spend most of her career trying to overcome the deep-rooted panic she felt that night. This accomplished winner of almost every accolade, from Tonys to Emmys, actually refrained from appearing on stages for almost thirty years. When she finally returned to the frontline in the 1990s, she never made a public appearance without a teleprompter and has been vocal about her performance anxiety hindering her craft. Having a prede-termined script became vital for her, and even as she wowed the audiences on the stage again, she worked hard to mask her inner turmoil.

A similar sense of mouth-drying dread can grip Christians when they think about having to share their faith, especially with those they know well. We feel we have to deliver an Oscar-winning performance every time, lest we somehow let down God and bring his kingdom to a grinding halt. But the side-by-side approach is not a stage-to-stage one.

To overcome this fear, I want to walk you through the Bible's version of a teleprompter that teaches us how to prepare for any conversation with those you are walking alongside. I like to call this helpful template the "Peter Pattern." First Peter 3:15 presents us with a pattern of preparation that frames our approach to the conversations we can have about Jesus. It encourages us to be ready, responsive, hopeful, and kind. Let's consider each of these in more detail for a moment.

Pattern 1: Be Ready

Always be ready. There is a Christian stereotype that assumes God opens up conversations about him only through rare divine opportunities. This is probably because we have heard many incredible stories from preachers that usually start with "I was sitting on a plane, and you will never guess what happened in conversation with the person next to me . . . " (By the way, why does God always use preachers on planes?)

A *divine appointment* is when God uniquely orchestrates circumstances for two or more people to meet in a specific way for a specific conversation that is clearly prearranged by God's hand. The Bible records many of these special appointments, such as the story of Philip and the eunuch in Acts 8:26–40, and we should be open to them. While still being expectant for occasional divine interventions, we also need to prepare for God to move in our daily interactions.

There is an annoying, frustrating reality about the art of spiritual conversations. People always ask questions at their convenience and rarely at yours. Anyone who has ever parented teenagers knows that they always want to talk late at night or when you have your hands full with other things. In the same way, we should expect the opportunities for connection to come when we least expect them. That is why we have to develop a pattern of preparation.

The first way we can prepare is to listen to God. Peter instructs us that we are to *revere Christ as Lord in our hearts,* which is an internal rhythm that can be formed only in the secret place of prayer, worship, and personal obedience. As we talk with people, we may notice a sense of God speaking to us, perhaps bringing something to the forefront of our imagination, or reminding us of a story we should share or a question we should ask. None of this will happen easily if we're not regularly listening to God before the conversation takes place.

The second way we can prepare is to listen to others around us. Listening is our secret weapon. Paying attention daily to what is being said, or even not said, helps us prayerfully prepare for that moment of opportunity. Listening helps us get to know others better for who they are, and it enables us to spot the signs of whether they're moving toward or away from God. As you listen through your daily interactions, you can be prayerfully inquisitive about where people are really at.

So, what might we be looking out for when we listen to people? One popular evangelism training resource identifies five interweaving themes that are considered to be key motivators in people's lives.

- *Theme 1:* Peace, satisfaction, or freedom from anxiety.

- *Theme 2:* Success, significance, or finding one's purpose in life.

- *Theme 3:* Love, friendship, or freedom from loneliness.

- *Theme 4:* Security, forgiveness, or an overall sense of well-being.

- *Theme 5:* Joy, happiness, or enjoyment of life.[1]

Although you might say that everyone wants *all* these things, there is often a major driver that shows up consistently, depending on the person you're walking with. What are the people with whom you engage daily looking for? Do they seem to long for peace, freedom, or happiness more than anything else? Are they hoping for success or significance as a priority? Are safety and security their major concern? Once we recognize a consistent theme, then we can prayerfully and sensitively share how Jesus offers lasting fulfilment. It starts with listening.

Pattern 2: Be Responsive

Give an answer. When we're asked about our faith, it's so easy to fudge a response. We can either be too busy or embarrassed to speak out, or we go over the top with our own agenda and script, seeing it as our one chance to drop a truth bomb.

Peter instructs us to be prepared to give answers when questions are asked. This is appropriate in most environments, even in the workplace where increasingly there are barriers to sharing our faith. Answer the questions they ask you, not the ones you wish they had. Just as the timing of conversations will unlikely be at our convenience, the questions they ask us will probably not meet our criteria either. But answering questions is the fastest way to tackle preconceptions, myths, stereotypes, and barriers as part of *preparing the way.*

It often depends on the generation with whom you are connecting as to the questions and barriers you will face. It is possibly a generalization, but the older will probably ask more logical questions while the younger will ask more lifestyle-based ones. Some of the classic logical questions could include:

- Why are there evil and suffering in our world?

- Why should the Bible have any authority today?

- How can Jesus be the only way to God?

- Aren't science and religion opposed to each other?

A more lifestyle-based approach to questioning may be:

- Why does God care about who I have sex with?

- Why does the Bible have such outdated rules?

- Why are Christians such hypocrites about money?

There are many books and resources that can help us deal with the common objections and questions about the Christian faith, from sexuality to suffering, but here I want to focus on the principle of not *what* you say but *how* you respond. Of course, if we don't know the answer, it's fine to say, "I don't know, but let's find out together."

We need to learn to ask questions about the questions we're being asked. Is this coming from the person's *head* or *heart*? If it's coming from their head, then it likely requires a logical response. If it's coming from their heart, then it requires a pastoral one. For example, someone may ask you, "Why does God allow suffering?" (which could be a head question) when what they really mean is "Why did God let my sister die of COVID-19?" (a heart question).

You can see how important it is to discern the difference and how complex it can get if we're not prepared in advance. Jesus was a master of discerning the question behind the questions he was being asked. But if you're in doubt about someone's motive, just politely respond, "Why did you ask that question?"

The words we use really matter. For example, when I say the word *church*, I picture the loving community where I have found friendship, inspiration, love, and support. Others, however, might immediately associate the word *church* with something altogether different. The word is often analogous with dogmatic, dry, boring religion, or it triggers a lack of trust in authority because of well-known corrupt pastors and shady priests. Words are always loaded. If we don't use our words wisely, then we may be putting up barriers rather than handing out invitations.

My wife was recently trying to resolve an issue with her online grocery shopping order. As she was talking to customer service, they kept using random terminology such as, "We have to repack your ambient items." In describing her experience afterwards, she said something that stuck with me: "I knew they were trying to help me, but I didn't understand what they were saying to each other, so it made me feel like an outsider." This is a perfect analogy for how we can turn off the very people we're trying to support when we alienate them with our *Christianese*. Always be ready—but try not to be weird!

Pattern 3: Be Hopeful

Stay in hope. People will want to inquire about your life, not because they think you have the right answer to their doctrinal question, but because you show a unique level of hope. There are so many reasons why we can choose to be cynical, critical, or discouraged, which is why it's so important to keep our hearts full of hope. The way you act as a role model for hope every single day makes every question point to Jesus.

Your personal story of hope plays a powerful role in directing people to Christ. When shared in a non-awkward, appropriate, and consensual way, our testimony does more than just pass on information to people: it supernaturally prepares the way for listeners to take their own steps toward Jesus.

In his seminal book *Living Proof,* Jim Peterson asserts that hope must be foundational to what we share because it becomes a gateway to deepening both love and faith:

> People are attracted by our *hope.* As they come closer in for a better look, our *love* disarms them, removing the would-be barriers and judgments. Bearing all things, believing all things, and enduring all things, it makes a bona fide relationship possible. In this context, as we explain our hope, and exercise our love from Christ, people are led into *faith.*[2]

There is no greater story of hope than the gospel itself. We must become confident in sharing the truth about God's love for us, humanity's problem in connecting with God, and Jesus' provision for us as the way back to life. As we become adept at translating and connecting this story with our audience, we can help people see how they can take a clear step toward Jesus.

Since we rarely have time to tell our entire story, it's probably helpful to practice how to share short and specific highlights that apply to the person with whom we're engaging. Jesus was comfortable in leaving people wanting more because he knew it was the Holy Spirit who would continue to do the work after the conversation had ended.

We often think that we have nothing to share about in our own lives, especially if we don't have an obvious big sudden transformation. We feel we have to present a picture-perfect solution about our lives to others that goes something like, "I was terrible and then I met Jesus and now everything is brilliant." But one of the core principles of discipleship is that every person has a process. You don't have to be perfect to share your hope. It's okay to share about your current struggles and how God is helping you through them. It's okay to be a work in progress yourself and share that you're still on a journey marked by hope. This really helps the listener recognize that everyone is on a journey, even after they come to Christ.

The goal is not just to leave a listener feeling inspired, comforted, or even impressed, because these are all emotions that fade. Talking in terms of your personal process of discovering God is always helpful, especially in the pre-discipleship stage. If you can decode and explain the steps you took toward Christ, then it's more likely to create a call to action. We ought to leave someone with a practical *next step* they could take after hearing our story. Consider asking a fellow Christian the following:

- What was your life like before Christ? What steps did you take to connect with Jesus?

- How did you become a Christian? What steps did you take to do this?

- What happened after you became a Christian? What steps did you take to grow in your faith?

As a way of practicing this, we might consider first creating space for sharing these kinds of hopeful journey-oriented stories with one another inside the church walls to help us flex our storytelling muscles beyond them.

Pattern 4: Be Kind

Act with gentle respect. Our words are powerful enough that they can help move people toward Jesus or away from him. When dealing with the gap between Christians and culture, tough conversations will inevitably happen. We are increasingly becoming wary of navigating tricky topics and therefore can avoid challenging conversations because of the risks of "cancel culture." But Jesus knew that navigating adversity would be part of what it means to make disciples. In these choppy cultural waters, kindness is key.

There is no greater place where kindness is needed than in the world of social media. When having conversations online, there are some unique things we need to consider to keep them from becoming toxic. It's much easier to take online conversations out of context, which means we have to be even more aware of our voice and tone. We have to be careful not just about *what* we are saying, but also about to *whom* we are talking. Trolls often have a hidden agenda to provoke and irritate people in the name of disruption and fun. We need to remember that there's a real person behind the avatar, so it's best to handle negativity with grace.

Although it's a place fraught with risk, there are some wonderful opportunities for us to start conversations online that can lead to moments of digital discipleship. For instance, someone had an online post with the amazing title "How to make Jesus interesting when cat videos exist." Aside from the fact that someone should give that person an award for that title, the post contains some really helpful advice about sharing your faith online.

It starts by reminding us that rather than get sucked into a time vortex, we can use social media to converse and connect with others:

> You have to offer something the algorithm can't, no matter how smart it gets: genuine human connection and understanding. Remember that the algorithm is basically an entertainment band aid that distracts people from their real problems and needs.
>
> Tricky life circumstances? Watch some YouTube instead.
>
> Mental health struggles? Read some funny memes instead.
>
> Mum battling cancer? Escape on TikTok for a while.[3]

It then encourages us to share why Jesus is our hope. When Christ becomes the genuine solution to our desires, needs, fears, and hopes, we must learn how to share *why*. This makes our online connections resonate with our offline lives. As the last part of the post says:

> When we share the gospel as just information, cat videos always win. BUT. When the Gospel meets human needs, we can beat the algorithm.

Christ always trumps cat videos. There is a rule of life found in Romans 12:14–19 that is world changing in its real-world application but especially relevant for tackling online conversations, interactions, and engagements. Here's how the Message puts it:

> "Bless your enemies; no cursing under your breath. Laugh with your happy friends when they're happy; share tears when they're down. Get along with each other; don't be stuck-up. Make friends with nobodies; don't be the great somebody. Don't hit back; discover beauty in everyone. If you've got it in you, get along with everybody. Don't insist on getting even; that's not for you to do. 'I'll do the judging,' says God. 'I'll take care of it.' "

Wouldn't our online and offline world be a kinder place if we all put this into practice?

Jesus modeled responding to uncomfortable conversations and conflict by practicing forgiveness and choosing to love beyond difference. The Holy Spirit helps us adopt an attitude of empathy, humility, and curiosity. We can be kind and stay connected despite our differences. We can learn to disagree well.

If we deal with people in a judgmental and harsh manner, then we end up simply reinforcing the stereotype that all Christians are narrow minded. We become part of the problem. Yet when faced with people who think differently from us, it doesn't mean we need to compromise or water down the heart of what we want to say.

Differences can open us up to new ideas, even ones on which we don't see eye to eye with others. We have to be open to change our own perspectives, not just try to persuade others to adopt ours. If you think about it, every conversation carries an element of risk because it might also change the way we see something. Openness is not about shifting the core of what we believe about Jesus, but it can definitely be about changing our preconceptions about the person we're trying to reach. Conversations remind us that we're not always right about everything! Therefore, we need to stay kind.

Not everyone will be ready to accept Jesus as their Lord and Savior in every moment of conversation, and that's okay. We need to trust the Holy Spirit as the leader in this process, not us. You won't ever be able to argue with someone to twist their arm toward Christianity. There is an element of persuasion, but never coercion. It is the Holy Spirit who does the convicting. But don't take it for granted that someone will know what to do next after you've had a conversation with them about Jesus. We need to leave people with next steps and clear calls to action.

Conversations as catalysts for someone taking another step toward God sound like:

> "May I invite you for a coffee to talk about this further?"
>
> "Here is a book or article I think you may like about the topic we were talking about."
>
> "This podcast is well worth a listen to."
>
> "May I introduce you to my friend who I really think you'll get on with?"
>
> "Do you have access to a Bible? If not, may I help you download it on your phone?"
>
> "Have you ever watched this online series about Jesus?"
>
> "Do you want to come to a party with me and meet some of my Christian friends?"
>
> "If I invited you to an Alpha Course, a place where you can explore questions about faith, would you come along and try it out with me?"

"Fancy a visit to a church service with me soon?"

"May I pray for you?"

Although these are tangible next steps, none of them will succeed long term without the fuel of prayer before, during, and after that moment of conversation. If we put the Peter Pattern into practice as the foundation of all our engagements about Christ, then both we and the person with whom we're talking are empowered. That's why it is so transformational.

REFLECT

Consider the four parts of the Peter Pattern:

- *Be ready.*
- *Be responsive.*
- *Be hopeful.*
- *Be kind.*

How can you put these more into practice in your conversations this week?

10

TALKING

*Let your conversation be always full of grace, seasoned with
salt, so that you may know how to answer everyone.*

Colossians 4:6

In the final scene of the 2011 sentimental film *We Bought a Zoo*,
widower Benjamin Mee (played by Matt Damon) takes his two
children, Rosie and Dylan, to Little Dom's Diner to share with
them the story of where he first met his late wife. This was part of
them working through their grief together after losing a mother
and a wife.

"She was right there," Benjamin says to his kids enthusiastically, pointing to a now empty table in the restaurant. "This is
the moment where both of you became a possibility."

"I love that you are telling stories again," remarks the little girl
to her father, noticing the fresh hope in his demeanor.

"This is the story before the story," responds Benjamin, pointing rather excitedly to both Rosie and Dylan. "This is where *you*
and *you* begin."

Benjamin then reenacts his first encounter by walking past
the window of the diner, where he first laid eyes on the most
beautiful woman he had ever seen. He courageously took the
chance to strike up a conversation that changed his life.

"Excuse me," he said nervously to the stranger sitting at the
table alone. "Why would an amazing woman like you even talk
to someone like me?"

With a smile on her face, his soon-to-be wife responded with two simple words that began their journey together: "Why not?"

This emotional conclusion to the movie, played perfectly by Damon, resonates with an earlier conversation he'd had with his son about seizing a moment for making a connection with someone. "You know, sometimes all you need is twenty seconds of insane courage, just literally twenty seconds of embarrassing bravery, and I promise you something great will come of it."

The idea that one significant conversation can change our lives for the better would have resonated with the two people who walked with Jesus on the road to Emmaus that later caused the travelers to exclaim, "Were not our hearts burning within us while he talked with us on the road and opened the Scriptures to us?" (Luke 24:32).

Conversations really matter. They are relational exchanges where ideas, information, stories, and experiences are explored together in a manner that leads to deeper relationships, changing perceptions, and sense-making. Conversations help you connect the dots, usher in aha moments, and help you work out what's really important to you.

In an interview about her book *Reclaiming Conversation*, Professor Sherry Turkle talks about conversation as the gateway to human intimacy:

> Conversation is the most human and humanizing thing that we do. It's where empathy is born, where intimacy is born—because of eye contact, because we can hear the tones of another person's voice, sense their body movements, sense their presence. It's where we learn about other people.[1]

Intimate conversations that place Jesus as the focus can cause people's humanity to come alive, their hearts to burn, perspectives to change, and lives to be transformed.

In the craziness of life, it often feels that our ability to hold meaningful conversations is waning. We are becoming less expectant about having interesting interactions about Christ because it seems that we barely talk about anything significant anymore. So, why have we lost the art of spiritual conversations? There are three obvious contenders for why this may be the case.

Challenge 1: Too Tech Driven

The first challenge is that we have become so technology driven.

The next time you go into a restaurant, look around at all the couples blatantly not talking to each other while they scroll on their phones. In a recent *Psychology Today* article, Susannah Newsonen cites the rise of the mobile phone as the main reason why people no longer talk to each other in person.

> Most people check their phone about 150 times a day—or every six minutes. Scarily, about 46% of people say they couldn't live without their smartphones. In an unplugged study done by the University of Maryland, one in three people said they'd rather give up sex than give up their smartphones.[2]

Our technological revolution is reducing communication to bite-sized, emoji-driven, quick-fire information sharing. While technology can give us the illusion that we're connected, we miss out on body language, tone, inflection, nuance, and the chemical bonding that happens with physical proximity.

Sometimes, we have to put down our tech if we want to turn up the volume of our conversation.

Challenge 2: Too Agenda Driven

The second challenge is that we have become so agenda driven.

In our personal lives, we have the daily grind of chores, family responsibilities, and work. But perhaps nowhere is the agenda-driven-ness of our culture more prevalent than in our churches. Our gatherings have become so agenda driven that they barely leave any breathing space for authentic engagement with others to take place. Congregants turn up just in time for a meeting, ready to sit side by side as an audience with others. They wait for the singing to start so they can enjoy a personal connection with God and then passively listen to a one-way talk. Afterwards, even if one stays for coffee, the chitchat often stays in the shallows of "How was your week?" or endless cycles of "I'm fine thanks—how are you?" And then it begins all over again the following Sunday with nothing in between.

Because of this, we have many Christians who are barely connecting with one another inside the church, let alone reaching non-Christians beyond it. We have forgotten how to talk in church. Prioritizing the margin and space needed for human connection in both our church programs and our personal lives is vital for ministry and mission. Inside the church, perhaps this starts by spending more time in a circle than we do in a row. Outside the church, it means being willing to be brave enough to stretch beyond small talk.

Challenge 3: Too Results Driven

The third challenge for us is that we have an expectation of immediate results.

Because of our instant consumer society and our anxious need to prove our ministry's success, we often dismiss the value of spiritual conversations because they don't always get someone to sign on the dotted line.

To counter this, I like to focus on having what some people call "nudge chats" with those around me. These are small simple nudges in our daily interactions that help provoke curiosity, encourage a sense of purpose and meaning, or inspire hope. They are the everyday moments that add flavor to our conversations, adding up to more than the sum of their parts when we infuse them with prayer and a lifestyle that prompts people to ask questions.

As an example of this, I was taking time to listen to two colleagues talk about a stressful situation that was going on at work.

As I chatted with them, I shared a little about how I deal with pressure when it comes my way. "You know what Jesus said about worry, don't you?" I asked with a grin on my face.

Turns out they didn't.

"He said don't worry about tomorrow," I continued, "for tomorrow will worry about itself."

"Interesting," one of them responded, slightly impressed at the relevance of Christ's words for a work context.

Then I completed the phrase with the sting in its tail: "Because each day has enough trouble of its own."

I could tell one of them was thinking "I was hoping Jesus would be slightly more inspiring than this," so I finished by saying something like: "Whenever I get up in the morning, I think about what today's trouble will be. I know there will be challenges right now, but they probably won't be the same ones tomorrow, so there's no point in letting them rule my life. The verse reminds me that I can always get through what comes at me today."

There is no dramatic end to this story except that it reminds us that small nudge talks can lead to minor changes in perceptions. The results are never up to us.

Three Habits of Open Conversation

There are three habits we can develop that help us avoid the traps of being distracted by technology, sidetracked by our agenda, or blinded by the desire for quick results.

HABIT 1: ASK OPEN QUESTIONS

Better questions always result in better conversations.

When I worked on the shop floor at Toys "R" Us as a teenager, I became the top bike seller because I put into practice what I was taught about the value of asking open-ended questions. Instead of saying "May I help you?" to which you would normally get a straight yes or no answer, they trained me to ask, "What kind of bike are you looking for?" This caused the customer to ponder for a minute because they couldn't just give a pat answer.

Open questions invite people to engage.

Jesus knew this, which is why on the road to Emmaus, he didn't approach the disciples and ask, "Do you want to hear what I have to say?" which is essentially a yes or no answer. He opened up the chat by asking, "What are you discussing together as you walk along?"

There are a few observations worth making about this conversation on the road to Emmaus.

- Jesus started by asking questions about what they thought they already knew about him.
- Jesus reflected on current events to open up conversations about himself.
- Jesus wasn't afraid to challenge and address underlying barriers that were preventing the disciples from knowing the truth about him.

We can do the same as we connect with others. When using open-ended questions, you may start by adapting sentences like these:

- Tell me about . . .
- What is your understanding of . . .
- How do you deal with . . .
- What would you do if . . .
- Is it possible that . . .
- What is stopping you from . . .

Being open with your questions will mean you can have a confident dialogue and not default to a critical monologue. It will amaze you at how seemingly mundane questions can open up deeper discussions in an environment where people feel comfortable and trust is fostered.

HABIT 2: LISTEN WITH OPEN EARS

Listening is at the heart of all effective conversations.

In my work as the operations director of Grace Foundation, I have had the privilege of having access to executive coaching via my business mentor Elaine. Coaching is a tool not just for when things are going wrong, but also for the personal development of high-potential leaders who manage growing organizations, especially during times of transition.

Coaching is incredibly, annoyingly brilliant. The focus is always on the coachee. Elaine hardly says a word. She is a "question ninja" and always seems to ask the right thing at the right time. In one hour, she can ask two or three killer questions and then reflect to me what I said in a way that helps me form my own next steps and see everything from a fresh perspective. I honestly don't know how she does it. When I talk to her, it's somehow like talking to myself.

There are some skills I have seen modeled by Elaine that have helped me improve my ability to listen well. First, always pay attention and show that you value what others have to say. Maintain eye contact and limit verbal judgments, avoiding interruptions. Wait for a pause in the flow and then ask clarifying questions if you need to. Whenever you are actively listening, pay attention to what is not being said as much as what is. Focus on nonverbal cues. Don't be afraid of silence. Remember, listening is not about staying quiet long enough so you can say what you want to say. Often reflecting back what has been said is enough to cause the coachee to say out loud, "Why on earth do I believe that?" Listening is that powerful.

Habit 3: Create Open Spaces

Life offers rare moments where we get to talk about the subjects we really care about.

Deeper conversations often spring up in the *in-between and informal* spaces. Depth rarely happens in strictly agenda-driven settings like work or in education. It happens around a meal table, around a campfire, or on a car journey. This means we have to slow down our timetable if we're to be intentional about going deeper with people.

Creating space in the margins lets us go beyond small talk that's driven by snippets of information exchange such as, "Nice weather we're having today." Small talk, however, is not always a bad thing. It's actually a useful form of bonding ritual that helps us develop trust, affirm positive intentions, and build chemistry. The natural order of most conversations is to start shallow and then move toward depth. You probably won't have many deep discussions until you have a deeper level of trust.

But there is more for us. This doesn't mean we have to artificially steer the conversation toward the things of God. Intentional space often speaks for itself. We are hard-wired to go deeper when we ask the right questions that tap into our emotional and spiritual well-being.

Back in 2016, I co-created a set of short Kleer Series videos (www.kleerseries.com) to help young people start conversations about spirituality, identity, choices, life, purpose, and faith in group contexts. The first session of the Kleer Series had a learning outcome that was simply, "Life is worth stopping to think about." At the end of that session, we ask young people to explore three simple questions, of which the first one is: "What does the idea that life is worth stopping to think about mean to you?"

There's no mention of God, Jesus, faith, or church in the first instance. In fact, we intentionally structured Kleer Series material so that there's no mention of the word *God* until Session Twenty to allow for a longer buildup of pre-discipleship-style engagement. But when I spoke to youth groups about how they were getting on with the videos, they often told me about the richness of conversations they were having about Christ and faith from earlier in the process.

"What session are you in, then?" I asked one group leader, after hearing the depth of discussion they'd just had, assuming they were near the end.

"Oh, we are still on Session One! Our young people just started asking questions about faith because they had time to slow down enough to think about it."

Creating intentional space for conversation is so powerful. When framed in an honest, open, inclusive environment, asking all kinds of spiritual questions can open up massive opportunities for spiritual growth. In talking about everything that matters, we end up talking about the one thing that really matters.

Pray for Open Opportunities

A surefire way we can put pre-discipleship into practice is to have conversations with people outside of the church about spiritual matters. While we can spend countless hours talking about things that don't matter at all, we all know the value of making our words count. Nothing moves a person down the line from being *not interested* to becoming *spiritually curious* faster than a Christ-centered conversation. Perhaps we ought to dedicate more of our prayer life to ask God to give us these opportunities, and then orient the rhythms of our life in a way that increases the chance that they can happen.

To invite someone to take a next step in their journey through the power of a conversation often takes risk from us. It takes bravery, discernment, and wisdom. But as Benjamin said earlier, "Sometimes all you need is twenty seconds of insane courage, just literally twenty seconds of embarrassing bravery, and I promise you something great will come of it."

Having conversations about Jesus is always a gateway to a grand adventure. It makes human hearts burn in a way that nothing else will. We may ask God, "Why would you ever use broken imperfect people like us for the worthy task of pointing others to Christ?"

But God just looks at us and says, "Why not?"

REFLECT

- *Which of the three drivers—being too tech driven, agenda driven, or results driven—hinders you in deepening the level of your conversations right now?*

- *Which of the three habits—asking open questions, listening with open ears, or creating open spaces—could you focus on to help you foster more spiritual conversations?*

11

TRANSLATING

And how can they believe in the one of whom they have not heard?

Romans 10:14

Sometimes, things we can't see hinder our conversations.

When I was eighteen, I was standing in a makeshift marquee somewhere in Germany about to preach the gospel to a group of young people when my nerves almost got the best of me. My inexperience as a public speaker was exacerbated because everything had to be done through a German interpreter. I was not exactly brilliant, but fortunately my translator was outstanding.

Every couple of sentences, I watched as the translator retold my stories and reshared my Scripture passages with mirrored intonation. Highlights included me trying to express to the crowd that God knows every hair on their head while accidentally pointing to a bald man (the interpreter wasn't sure what to do with that one). At the end of my talk, a German pastor came out and basically re-preached the entire thing so that it made more sense.

Since this false start, I have spoken through interpreters all over the world and have learned to love the rapport I can build with others in this way. If you think about it, all good communication needs to be interpreted for the audience we're trying to reach anyway, even if we're speaking the same language. Resonance lies at the heart of effective communication.

One of the defining steps in the discipleship journey is when someone first hears about Jesus and the good news. It's only through hearing the gospel that we can move from having no awareness of God, and being uninterested or disengaged, to moving to the point of spiritual curiosity and beyond. Without the clear step in which people hear and respond to the good news, there can be no engagement in authentic discipleship later down the road. As Paul says in Romans 10:14,

> How, then, can they call on the one they have not believed in? And how can they believe in the one of whom they have not heard? And how can they hear without someone preaching to them?

In this verse, you can trace the journey from hearing to believing to walking. Over the centuries, Christians have used countless methods to proclaim the good news—from the prose of the priest to the paper of the printing press. Some of these approaches have stood the test of time, while others have fallen by the wayside. For example, fuzzy felt (otherwise known as a flannelgraph), believe it or not, was once considered a revolutionary evangelistic strategy. Standing on a street corner, storytellers would use a board covered with flannel fabric to communicate Bible stories to passers-by (some of us remember these flannel boards from our Sunday school classes). While there's clearly nothing wrong with this method, it may not meet a "felt need" (excuse the pun) of the digital generation.

Nowadays, ever-changing forms of digital technology are used as vehicles for sharing the gospel. Of course, you can still have a good old-fashioned conversation with another human being too! While most people would agree that we need to adapt our medium for a modern audience, some argue that we also need to think about changing our message. This may seem blasphemous to those who put their trust in an unchanging gospel. Yet, while truth is always timeless, we need to think about the way we present and position it in culture that constantly tries to muffle the good news.

When I was a kid, I went on a school trip to a performance of Shakespeare's *Richard III*, performed by a troupe of Romanian actors who delivered it enthusiastically in their native language. To be honest, this had a niche appeal to a group of English-speaking students. Perhaps the most memorable part was when the lights suddenly went off, rain started falling on stage, and a drenched wolf came out of nowhere and howled at a bunch of schoolchildren! To this day, I don't know what that experience was about. The play suffered from a serious lack of understanding of its audience, an inhospitable language barrier, and a severe lack of clarity over why anyone should even be there to engage with it. Sadly, I fear that many people's experiences of church ends up with a similar list of problems.

Many of those we are trying to reach can actually leave our church services without grasping our language, knowing how to connect with us, or understanding why they even went there in the first place. They leave with culture shock.

The danger for us is that we use so many Christian buzzwords and religious terminology and jargon that we don't actually communicate anything at all. As one example of how this can play out, I remember observing a first-time visitor in a church service sitting with her Christian friend and looking nervous about what she was about to experience. As the singing started, the visitor slowly looked more confused and disengaged. Meanwhile, the Christians in the room became more passionately engaged as they sang "Reckless Love" by Cory Asbury:

Oh, the overwhelming, never-ending reckless love of God. . . .
Oh, it chases me down, fights 'til I'm found, leaves the ninety-nine.

I listened as she turned to her friend and whispered, "Why does God want to leave ninety-nine people behind?" Having never heard the parable of the lost sheep, she wondered why a God, who would abandon so many people out of a hundred, was worth worshiping.

It was interesting to see how 99 percent of the room was loving it, and yet the 1 percent really struggled to connect. Why? Because of unfamiliar words and phrasing. To the uninitiated, our religious language is often confusing and obscure. Thankfully, for the visitor's sake, we weren't singing about how our God is both a lion and a lamb! It's also worth commenting that that the friend was ready to act as a guide.

One of the most interesting phrases I've picked up from education theory is called the "curse of knowledge." This is basically when an individual tries to communicate something to others, assuming they have the background knowledge to grasp what's being said. This is born from the inability of teachers to put themselves in the shoes of the learners. They are simply too far ahead in the process and cannot decode the steps for others.

I believe we see the "curse of knowledge" ever present in the church in the way we disciple new believers inside the church and evangelize those beyond it. This is one of the primary reasons our message and methods fail to resonate.

On Mute or on Message?

One of the awkward parts of the technological transition to lockdown life during the early stages of the global pandemic was moving meetings online via Zoom or Microsoft Teams. I've lost count of the times my colleagues at work started a video call with at least one person (usually the same guy) talking emphatically while the rest of the team shouted repeatedly, "You're on mute! YOU ARE ON MUTE!" This is basically what communication is like between the church and the world beyond its walls. Although we may talk with passion, no one can hear what we have to say. But in the case of the church, no one on the other end is bothering to tell us that they can't hear.

We need to move from being on mute to being on message.

This is harder than ever when our voice is so dampened by the surrounding culture. If you've ever tried to speak to a friend in a room filled with loud music, then you know what it's like to communicate the gospel in a culture that constantly drowns you out. If culture can be that much of a barrier to our gospel amplification, then that's why we need to understand it.

In his famous graduation speech, "This Is Water," the writer David Foster Wallace began with a parable:

> There are these two young fish swimming along, and they happen to meet an older fish swimming the other way, who nods at them and says, "Morning, boys. How's the water?" The two young fish swim on for a bit, and then eventually one of them looks over at the other and goes, "What the hell is water?"[1]

He later stated that, "The point of the fish story is merely that the most obvious, important realities are often the ones that are hardest to see and talk about."[2] Culture is the water in which we're all swimming while not even realizing we're wet.

Our culture tells stories, raises questions, and creates narratives that can hinder or help people hear the good news of Jesus. If we don't understand the times in which we're living, then our message won't resonate even if it is true. There are therefore three aspects we ought to grasp about culture that will help us translate the good news into it.

ASPECT 1: CULTURE MAKES US PROMISES

I first engaged with the study of culture while training to be a graphic designer in the early 2000s. While researching consumer culture, I realized the words seemed to compete with themselves. "Consumer" means "to use up" and "culture" means "to grow." So, the literal translation of "consumer culture" is "to grow something by using it up," which is an impossible paradox. Herein lies the heart of our problem with modern life!

As I studied, I noticed a correlation emerge between consumerism and religion. Consumerism can define a person's identity, value, and activity, which makes it more than just practical—it can become spiritual. There is a divine-like status attributed to anything that offers people enlightenment and deliverance. You can almost imagine shopping malls as the new cathedrals, brands as the new commandments, debt as the new sin, and so on.

Consumerism is no longer just about meeting our physical needs; otherwise, there would be more than enough stuff to go around for everyone. Perhaps this endless search for identity is why we can't ever seem to stop consuming new things?

This whole area of culture fascinated me to the point that I chose it as the subject of a ten-thousand-word essay I had to write as part of my university degree. Among my peers, my title was legendarily long: "An Examination of the Generally Accepted Meanings of the Cross in Christian Symbolism and How Those Meanings Are Expressed through a Postmodern Consumer Culture."

The essay was a study about how the physical object of the cross had been devalued in a postmodern, post-Christian culture to become an empty fashion symbol. It was seen as something to wear at the weekend, a weapon to ward off vampires in movies, or a representative of an archaic institution. While the object itself became irrelevant to those outside the church community, the original meaning of deliverance became more desired in culture than ever.

To the first disciples, that cross was a sign of hope for deliverance. It was the belief that it could set them free from the state they were in and bring them into something new. Perhaps every single aspect of consumer culture tries to offer us the same thing today:

- Buy this product and you will be truly happy.

- Wear this symbol and you will find new status or identity.

- Live this lifestyle and you will be free.

The new symbols of deliverance are everywhere. We have to come to our own conclusion about whether the equation of *Cons (u + me) rs* is working. Only through the burden of feeling empty can we reassess our need for a deliverance that lasts. When we see the constant empty promises of deliverance, the cross suddenly becomes relevant again. While that's a whistle-stop summary of a ten-thousand-word essay, it's a reminder that deliverance never goes out of fashion in any culture.

As we share the good news of the gospel, we start to help people join the dots and find Jesus as their source of hope and deliverance. His promises are everlasting.

ASPECT 2: CULTURE TELLS US STORIES

A cultural narrative is defined as the "overlearned stories communicated through mass media or other large social and cultural institutions and social networks."[3] I love the phrase "overlearned story" as it speaks of how ingrained some ideas are in our world to where we rarely question if they are true.

We live in a generation that has been sold out on narratives that place fame, money, technological progress, power, or sex as the idols of our potential deliverance. While culture promises so much and yet delivers so little, Jesus tells a different story.

Pastor and author John Mark Comer advocates for an approach to evangelism that takes the key messages propagated by any culture and tests them against the truth of the gospel. While talking about this in a recent podcast, he said:

> It's like Philip Rieff's whole thing, that sociologist. He said, "The best way to critique secular culture is to biopsy it." I really like that word. Think of a biopsy. You just cut out a little piece and you hold it up under the light and put it under a microscope.[4]

We can hold up an aspect of a culture's version of the good news and see if it becomes fake news when exposed to the light.

Buying into the stories that culture tells us is not a harmless pastime like believing a fairy tale; they consume our time, energy, and effort, filling every chapter of our lives. Jesus knew how caught up in their own narratives people were, which is why he told disruptive parables that were minor stories or counternarratives In order to break this cycle, we have to translate the gospel in the light of how consumed people are by the culture they are so caught up in. Unless people start to question the narratives they believe, they will rarely want to change or move out of it. When this happens, it the spiritual equivalent of the human battery Neo finding out he's part of the Matrix run by highly advanced technical machines.

Perhaps the reason we're so quick to believe stories that aren't true is because they provide temporary solutions to the unanswered questions we have about ourselves. For example, the big three giants of sex, money, and power are idols we cling to because they fulfill a deeper human need to feel loved, to feel safe, and to feel like we're enough. So, we need to ask: What are the real questions our culture is trying to find answers for?

How would you fill in these blanks for the type of audience you're trying to reach if you wanted to expose them to the good news?

- Sex offers_____, but Jesus is_____.

- Money offers_____, but Jesus is_____.

- Power offers_____, but Jesus is_____.

In his own approach to sharing faith, Pastor Tim Keller from New York puts it like this: "You've actually got to find a way to take the plot line of the culture and give it a happy ending in Jesus."[5] This feels like a helpful starting point by which to frame the gospel for those with whom we're walking because it scratches where they're itching. It comes from their starting point and not ours.

Aspect 3: Culture Offers Us Answers

A traditional flow of a gospel presentation, whether shared one to one or from a stage, usually goes something like this: "God loves you, but you live apart from God. Jesus died for you, so you need to decide to follow Jesus." What's wrong with this, I hear you say? Absolutely nothing. It's the total truth, but the way we communicate it to our audience really matters. Context should always dictate content. It's not just about sharing facts, but about prayerfully thinking through how the truth might resonate with others. Subtle differences in communication make a big impact.

While previous generations asked questions like "How do I get to heaven?" or "What do I do with my guilt?" younger generations now ask entirely different questions, such as "What does it mean for me to thrive as a human being?"

Knowing how people find answers to their deepest questions helps us adapt the communication of our gospel message without losing its essence. In their book *3 Big Questions That Change*

Every Teenager, Dr. Kara Powell and Brad Griffin identify three key questions that motivate teenagers in modern culture.

> 1. *Who am I?* Teenagers wrestle with what others expect them to be and often don't feel they're good enough. They feel defined by their outer image, but they long to be seen as more than a stereotype. How does our gospel speak into this? How does it tell them they are enough in God?
>
> 2. *Where do I fit?* Young people are looking for spaces where they feel safe to be themselves. They want to belong to a group of people where they share something in common and feel like they are needed. How does our gospel tell them that they belong here?
>
> 3. *What difference can I make?* Adolescents want to play an active part in changing the world. They don't want to sit on the sidelines, but they need someone to show them how to build a positive future for themselves and give them a sense of agency. How does the gospel we share invoke a sense of calling and purpose? [6]

What's helpful about these three questions on identity, purpose, and belonging from Powell and Griffin is not only that they give an insight into the next generation, but that they could almost be about any generation. If our framework for sharing the gospel doesn't at least attempt to answer one of these deeper longings, then it's likely to fall on deaf ears. We can't just hope that people make an abstract connection for themselves. We have to show and tell. In simple terms, we need to help people connect God's story with theirs.

The ultimate goal in being able to translate the gospel into our culture is that we can start to question culture itself.

- Do the promises that culture makes us come true?

- Do the stories that culture tells us add up?

- Are the answers that culture offers us worth considering?

Suddenly, the biggest barrier that's been holding us back becomes the greatest opportunity to reveal the good news.

- Our gospel makes promises it always keeps.

- The stories matter that God tells us.

- We always find an answer in Jesus.

As Christians, we need to become translators of truth. We need a framework that helps turn down the volume of culture and amplifies the message of the gospel (not the other way around). We need to paint a picture of Jesus that stirs people to come alive with the reality of who he is and who they can be with him. We need to share good news—not as a transactional statement that leads to an easy conclusion, but as a powerful invitation to find out more. After all, how can we ever start to make disciples if we don't even make sense?

REFLECT ════════════════════════════════

- *What would you say are the biggest promises, stories, and answers you see being shared in your surrounding culture?*

- *How might the gospel speak into this and actually offer good news?*

12

BEHOLDING

*And we all, who with unveiled faces contemplate the Lord's
glory, are being transformed into his image with ever-increasing
glory, which comes from the Lord, who is the Spirit.*

2 Corinthians 3:18

Passion is the driver of all our engaging conversations. Whether
it's the latest program, tech gadget, or new relationship, people
love to talk about what they love! What we are passionate about
gets talked about. And we love to share the things we are devoted
to with those we care about.

Pastor Jay Pathak, national director of Vineyard USA, has a
desire to move evangelism from the world of "being weird" to
being seen as "sharing what you love." He discusses this in one
of his online teaching sessions:

> When you love people well, you share what you love. You don't
> have to be trained to do this. You've probably been to a great res-
> taurant, and you talk about it with your friends. Nobody makes
> you do it. Or a band that you like, or even a flavor of ice cream.
> You tell people you've got to have this because you share natu-
> rally what you love.[1]

The key to spiritual curiosity starts with us. We can never au-
thentically help others discover a passionate love for Jesus if we
ourselves are uninterested and disengaged. Our religious apathy
and sense of monotony can sometimes become a blockage of the

very thing we want others to take hold of. We can lead people only where we've already been.

We may privately think to ourselves, "I already know all I need to know about Christ." This is called a fixed mindset rather than a growth one. You may have a locked-in impression of who Jesus is, but let me suggest this: If the disciples were *with* Jesus 24/7, and they still didn't know him fully, maybe there's more yet for us to know?

Paul the Apostle knew that Jesus was better than we think as he explains his role to the churches: "Although I am less than the least of all the Lord's people, this grace was given me: to preach to the Gentiles the *boundless riches* of Christ" (Ephesians 3:8; italics added). The word here for "boundless" may also be translated "unfathomable." This describes a Jesus who cannot be fully comprehended. There are no limits to the riches of Christ. If you think you can fathom Jesus, then you may not know him as well as you think you do. Try as we might, we can never plumb the depths of Christ's worth.

The beauty in Christ is found in the beholding of him!

To "behold" means to look intensely at something with great affection—it's so much more than a quick glance for a temporary fix. It is from this position of being transfixed by Jesus that we can start to reach out and share about the one we love. This is a far cry from most church outreach strategies that seem to extol the benefits of meetings before they unpack the beauty of Christ.

So many Christians end up like the kid who gets a present at Christmas and unwraps it, only to be more captivated with the box. We can become distracted by the pretty packaging of religion rather than keep the good news at the core of who we are and what we offer to people. We default to conversations such as:

- Would you like to come to my church meeting? You'll really like the coffee and music.

- Have you seen what good stuff my church is doing for the community?

- Can you see how my church agrees with you on this really important, culturally relevant issue?

There are many churches that offer great worship music, sound advice, and encouragement to help you through the week and a deep-spirited community with good social activities and friends. These things are fine in and of themselves, but they're not the gospel. Our interactions with those we're walking alongside must always focus more on Jesus than on religion. In his teachings, Pastor Sam Allberry reminds us that "we are not marketing a product; we are introducing people to a person."[2]

If Jesus is the way, the truth, and the life, then our message doesn't start with describing a church service. It starts with describing Christ. In Romans 1:16, Paul says, "For I am not ashamed of the gospel, because it is the power of God that brings salvation to everyone who believes." Where is the source of power in this verse?

- Relevant pastors won't save people.

- Great preaching won't save people.

- Emotional worship music won't save people.

- Serving every week on a ministry team won't save people.

- The power is in the good news about Jesus.

Too often, Jesus is reduced to a transaction rather than a relationship. We have to avoid the oversimplified version of the good news that basically tells others to "ask Jesus into their hearts" with only a brief explanation about who Christ is or what that statement actually means.

For those of us who have grown up in the church, our association with the word *Jesus* is positive, evoking a sense of gratitude and grace. I am so used to hearing the name "Jesus" that I forget it's only ever heard as a swear word to so many.

Jesus has a major image problem.

According to research by *Talking Jesus*, 40 percent of adults in the UK didn't realize that Jesus was a real person. Note the wording here: not *believed*; they simply *didn't realize*. Thirty per-cent of those who recognize him as historical believe that Jesus was a prophet or spiritual leader, but not God. Conversely, 43 percent believe in the resurrection of Jesus from the dead.[3] The most common words those outside the church use to describe Jesus include *loving, spiritual,* and *peaceful.* This leaves a door-way for discussion still open. We just have to know that someone else's starting point is going to differ vastly from our own, even when we feel like we're still getting to know Christ ourselves.

In one of our more recent Kleer Series videos, we focus on provoking discussion about who Jesus is. In these videos, we identify six key characteristics that help young people see a more three-dimensional, high-definition version of Christ that can help us focus our conversation after we discern where the person is at.

Focus 1: Jesus Is Real

For those who are skeptical, focus the conversation on the fact that Jesus is real.

One thing we need to help those outside the church under-stand about Jesus is that he is actually real. It would amaze you how many people treat Christ as if he's a myth like the Loch Ness monster. There's bountiful evidence that Jesus was a walk-ing, talking person who lived in the Middle East over two thou-sand years ago. Get to know some of the basic facts for yourself from books such as *The Case for Christ,*[4] and you will feel more equipped to tackle basic objections when they come.

People may hear about a baby Jesus at Christmas time and a dying Jesus at Easter, but the problem with just knowing the festival version of Jesus is that we learn about the beginning and end of his life with virtually nothing in between. This can rein-force the idea that we can put God in a religious box and pull him out on special occasions. But if we can help others see that Jesus really was part of our history, then that definitely gives them questions to consider for their future.

Focus 2: Jesus Is Relevant

For those who are disinterested, focus the conversation on the fact that Jesus is relevant.

The "He Gets Us" marketing campaign (www.hegetsus.com) was created to inspire cultural change in the way people think about Jesus and his relevance in our lives. Their video website smashed through 100 million views in the first four weeks of launch, making it one of the most successful digital outreach campaigns ever. Their purpose is to help modern skeptics realize the humanity of Jesus. It champions messages such as the following:

> *We all deal with rejection.* Whether you've been turned down for a job, ghosted after a first date, or even cast out by your own family, Jesus understands. He dealt with rejection too.
>
> *If you're struggling to make ends meet, you're not alone.* Even Jesus was born into poverty, and he struggled day to day to put food on his table.
>
> *Shame. Humiliation. Fear. A hollow sadness.* If you've ever been bullied, mocked, or harassed, you know these feelings well. What you may not know is that Jesus knew them too.

Although he is the most famous person in history, when someone hears the name "Jesus," many may not have a burning desire to follow in his footsteps. But that's probably because they've had a bad first impression of him. Some people's view of Jesus is formed through a three-second Google search. This reveals a caricature of Christ from ancient art or via pop-culture memes (often a white, Americanized Jesus associated with politics rather than faith). By showing that Jesus went through the same issues, problems, and emotions that we have, this campaign strives to resonate with where people are at. When we invite people to look beyond the stereotype, Jesus becomes more relevant than they realized.

Focus 3: Jesus Is God's Reflection

For those looking for answers about what God is like, focus the conversation on the idea that Jesus is God's reflection.

The image that springs to mind when we think of the word *God* is crucial when deciding how to respond to the good news. Perhaps people see a powerful creator, an angry dictator, or even just a distant spectator. Do they imagine an old man on a white cloud or an impersonal force? Maybe they see nothing at all. We live in a world of competing worldviews and ideologies, so we shouldn't assume that others see God the same way we do. Even the slightest differences in perception can leave room for miscommunication and misunderstanding. God knew this would be a problem even two thousand years ago, which is why he sent Jesus to answer the question once and for all about what God is really like. If God took a selfie, it would look like Jesus.

Focus 4: Jesus Is Our Rescuer

For those looking for hope and forgiveness, focus the conversation on the truth that Jesus is their rescuer.

One of the most common objections to Christianity is that the world is so messed up. Surely, if God exists, he would have done something about it by now? We only have to scroll on our newsfeed to see that things appear to be broken on a global scale. Most of us are desperate for some kind of solution, some kind of deliverance from sin, selfishness, and the structures that keep everyone oppressed. Perhaps the boldest claim Jesus made about himself was that he was, in fact, that rescuer. This was such a radical statement that it even cost Jesus his life. In a world full of suffering, God shows us how to overcome by trusting in the cross's power. Unpacking the meaning of the death and resurrection of Jesus is the heart of the good news.

Focus 5: Jesus Is a Revolutionary

For those looking for purpose, focus the conversation on the concept that Jesus is a revolutionary.

The Christian story is not just about fixing individuals but about changing the entire world. When we follow Jesus, we live out the purpose for which all humans were born. God rescued us to become part of a story that is bigger than all of us. This revolution has been the inspiration for educating children, establishing universities, and building hospitals. It has inspired people to found orphanages, create homes for the elderly, care for the poor, feed the hungry, and help the homeless. And this is a story that is not yet finished. We are all invited to play our part in God's plan to make everything new.

Focus 6: Jesus Offers Relationship

For those looking for a way out of isolation, focus the conversation on the reality that Jesus offers relationship.

In a world where loneliness has become a global pandemic, God offers us an invitation to intimacy. Jesus offers us a friendship unlike any other. In fact, Christians use the word *Emmanuel*, which can be translated as "God with us," to describe who Jesus is. This was why the first Christians were so full of hope, courage, and purpose; they knew they were no longer alone.

Refocusing on Jesus

Whether you're talking or sharing about the facts of Jesus in history or his relevance to humanity, every time you speak his name, it's making a difference, shaping thinking, changing perceptions, and preparing the way. Hearts burn and yearn as we lift up the name of Christ.

It's vital to remember that our inability to see Jesus for who he really is isn't just a practical or cultural problem; it's a spiritual one:

> He was in the world, and though the world was made through him, the world did not recognize him. He came to that which was his own, but his own did not receive him. (John 1:10–11)

Every conversation or moment of sharing about the one we love needs to happen in parallel with prayer in order to break this cycle of spiritual blindness. It's only through a revelation by God's Spirit that people can recognize Jesus for who he really is.

The pressing question for you to ask yourself in the meantime is when was the last time you took a fresh look at Jesus for yourself?

REFLECT ══

- *How can you take a fresh look at Jesus?*
- *What would it look like for you to share more about your passion for Christ with others?*

13

CREATING

For we are God's handiwork, created in Christ Jesus to do good works, which God prepared in advance for us to do.

Ephesians 2:10

Creativity can spark a conversation and shift perceptions like almost nothing else can.

Jessica Bond is a New Zealand born Catholic artist, wordsmith, and owner of the Salt & Gold Collection (https://saltandgoldstore .com). She brought Salt & Gold to life during the COVID-19 global pandemic with a motto about helping people discover "God in plain English." Her viral *Footwashing Series* book is a powerful set of illustrations depicting different types of people sitting on a stool while Christ lovingly washes their feet. The series title reads: "Be prepared for Jesus to flip the tables of your heart. It's not about who's on the seat; it's about Who's washing the feet."

The first time I scrolled through the book, I noticed several meaningful depictions of those I instinctively agreed needed a touch from Christ.

- A lonely girl needs comfort and to know she is loved.

- A homeless person needs to know they can find security.

- A prisoner needs to know they can find forgiveness and hope.

Although I began looking while still in my religious comfort zone, the pictures chipped away at my prejudice and challenged who I think deserves to sit on the stool.

A picture of Jesus washing the feet of celebrities Kanye West and Justin Bieber with the caption: "Pretty bold of me to make a judgment about whether someone is saved or not when that's Jesus' job. (Don't I just love the power trip though.)"

I start to feel uncomfortable.

Jesus washes the feet of a Ukrainian mother weary from war. He also washes the feet of the Russian soldier too. The soldier's face looks suspiciously like Putin. The caption reads: "I don't get to decide who is ready or worthy to sit on the stool."

Now I feel challenged.

Then comes the image of a young man from the LGBTQ+ community holding a rainbow flag having his feet cleansed by King Jesus. The caption (nervously posted at 2:00 am after much deliberation from the artist) includes the line: "He sees past the things we make our identity, and just loves us as his children."

I am reflective.

Finally, I see the image of two men that are instantly recognizable by their outline and gait. In the first, I see former US President Donald Trump being gently served by Jesus. The second shows President Joe Biden.

> All our caricatures of politics, polarized positions, and personalities collide with the humility of the man who even washed the feet of the one who would betray him with a kiss.

By now, I am fully confronted and exposed in an almost visceral way because of every media stereotype I have in my head about both men.

If a picture paints a thousand words, then more might be said about who Christ is through one image than by a thousand microphones on a thousand stages. Creativity is such a powerful but untapped tool for disciple-makers of all kinds. Creativity creates curiosity. It rails against our preconceptions and invites us to reconsider what we thought we knew. Creativity whispers to us to leave behind assumptions and step into the realm of imagination and possibility. As those who are made in the image of God, creativity is already in our DNA.

Want to make disciples? Make art.

In the iconic painting of *The Church at Auvers,* now at the Musee d'Orsay in Paris, we see a visual expression of Vincent van Gogh's complex relationship with religion, especially as his mental health deteriorated during his latter days. Van Gogh paints a gloomy, dark image of an inaccessible, inhospitable building trapped in the shadows and devoid of light. Some people have dubbed this painting *The Church with No Doors,* which could also be the title of a poignant preaching series about how we have locked out the very people God commissioned us to invite in! Sadly, van Gogh was not the last artist to feel like he didn't know where he fit into the church.

Typically, when we consider our church communities, we think of the limited ways that creative artists are allowed out of their box for outreach meetings at Easter or Christmas! Much of our creative energy, effort, and resource goes into the branding and aesthetic of our church services. We focus on making our programs slicker. While this has improved our own religious experience, it has limited our view of artistry as a tool for reaching others beyond the church doors. But creativity has always been a hidden powerhouse of a tool for mission, evangelism, and discipleship.

Nowadays, we have copies of the Bible available at the touch of a button and dozens of translations on our bookshelves, but it wasn't until the invention of the Gutenberg Press in 1455 that there was a way for the average person to hold Scripture in their hands. So how did people understand the story of God before they had it on their iPhones as the Bible App? Back in the day, they were reliant on second-hand sayings, curated sermons, retold stories, and historical songs, celebrations, and rhythms of life. But perhaps the most potent asset they had was art.

Art has always been a means of expressing identity, purpose, and belonging in church history from the catacombs to the cathedrals. At first, the creative symbols were coded, almost secretive and subversive among the backdrop of society: a fish, a peacock, a lamb, a Christogram, or an anchor whispered to us about Christ. They repurposed early depictions of Christ from paganism; like the Greek image of a young man carrying a lamb over his shoulder, previously used by many philosophies and religions, that became refocused as the Good Shepherd himself. Later, there was an explosion of art and artistry inspired by Christ that has shaped generations with the good news.

Art has been communicating the story of God long before the printed word ever could. With this in mind, there's something comforting for us to remember as the world ignores the Bible again: We can use the power of creativity to recapture lost attention and retell the story. As disciples, we can use our creative gifts and talents to:

- Harness creativity to help move people from being not interested to being spiritually curious.

- Signpost people to the gospel using words, pictures, expressions, and symbols—both implicit and explicit, secret and revealed.

- Offer a doorway to spiritual formation.

- Become a cultural change-maker.

We can use our creativity to help capture attention, cultivate spiritual literacy, and start conversations.

Use Your Creativity to Capture Attention

Think of it like this: Any creative output, expressed in any sphere of influence, is like a flint to a dry pile of wood and kindling. The spark from a creative moment or movement, when infused with the fuel of the Holy Spirit, can ignite something in a person's soul. Dr. Malcolm Yarnell speaks about how art can become a bridge to the gospel when we use it as a hook to start a spiritual conversation.

Our architecture, music, literature, paintings, jewelry, even the clothes we wear, can be an avenue to start gospel conversations and teach basic Christian doctrines. Try it. Although God himself can never be fully captured by human art, he may sovereignly decide to work through it, together with your voice, to draw people to Christ.[1]

This is not just limited to traditional paintings of an artist impression of Jesus. It can include something you create or something creative you share with others, such as:

- A song that stirs your emotions.
- A picture that captures your heart.
- A social media post that makes you think.
- A poem that causes you to ponder.
- A speech that moves you to take action.
- A photograph that stops you in your tracks.
- A film that challenges your perceptions.
- A book that stays with you for days.
- A fashion item with an engaging message.
- A sculpture that reminds you of something that may otherwise be forgotten.
- A play that invites you into a novel experience.
- A marketing campaign that gives you clear next steps.

The list of creative possibilities is endless. Although you may not see yourself as an artist, most people are more creative than they think. They often feel like they need permission to step out into it, but Jesus gave us that permission when he commissioned us to go.

Use Your Creativity to Cultivate Spiritual Literacy

We can define spiritual literacy as developing our ability to read sacred signs around us that point to evidence of a creator.

It's impossible to fully appreciate a Mark Rothko painting until you've been in proximity to one in real life. Just because you've seen a digital image doesn't mean you've seen a Rothko. You have to observe the scale of the piece in relation to your own body, drink in the color's depth with your eyes, and feel the texture of the canvas in your soul. Art curator Glenn Phillips describes this moving way of experiencing art as "The Rothko Experience."

> Rothko's work has variously been described as transcendental, tragic, mystical, violent, or serene; as representative of the void; as opening onto the experience of the sublime; as exhilaratingly intellectual; or as profoundly spiritual—to mention just a few examples.[2]

How can a few flecks of paint on a canvas be described as profoundly spiritual? Because art can't easily be pigeon-holed into our five senses. The philosophical heavyweights like Plato, Aristotle, Augustine, and Aquinas decided that there were at least three things that could be *transcendental*, meaning that they were considered to have a spiritual aspect beyond any concrete physical space and time. These three qualities are truth, beauty, and goodness. We yearn for truth, we long for beauty, and we desire goodness. Experiencing these can touch our souls in a way that makes us want to go deeper. When we see glimpses of this in art, music, poetry, literature, and architecture, it evokes a sense of fulfillment, inspiration, and awe. As we create something that reflects an aspect of truth, beauty, or goodness, we actually point to evidence for both a soul and a savior. Why? Because Jesus is the ultimate expression of truth, beauty, and goodness. When we understand that *all things* have been created *by* and *for* Jesus, it opens up a way for us to dedicate all the things we create *to* him.

Use the Creativity of Culture to Start Conversations

You don't have be the next van Gogh to make the most of creativity. We can easily harness content in popular culture such as film, television, music, lyrics, poetry, and plays to start spiritual conversations. We can point to what's seen in popular culture and invite people to consider what is unseen. Paul was a master of this, as modeled in Acts 17:22–33,

> Paul then stood up in the meeting of the Areopagus and said: "People of Athens! I see that in every way you are very religious. For as I walked around and looked carefully at your objects of worship, I even found an altar with this inscription: to an unknown god. So you are ignorant of the very thing you worship—and this is what I am going to proclaim to you."

Paul used the icons and slogans of the day to start with something they knew and introduce something they didn't. Our modern expressions of human creativity can act as a gateway to explore where the gospel themes of creation, fall, redemption, and new creation are playing out in society around us.

We can even use "water-cooler moments" to help people make connections to the gospel by talking with them about the deeper meaning behind entertainment such as:

- The superhero story dominating the movie theater.
- The lyrics in that love song topping the charts.
- The plotline in the latest book everyone is reading.
- That must-see television series.

It's a fun exercise to practice making cultural links to the gospel with groups of like-minded friends. Ask questions like what does Batman, Beatboxing, or Bollywood have to do with the gospel?

Using familiar icons, characters, or story beats can open up conversations about universal themes such as:

- Where do I find lasting peace and satisfaction?
- What is the purpose of life?
- How do I find my significance?
- What is the secret to intimacy in relationships?

- Where do I place my security and hope?

- How do I find happiness?

We can use these themes as hooks to explore how we find our solutions in Christ and the gospel story. As we have talked about promises, narratives, and answers from culture, there is no better place to challenge these than through examining the examples we find in modern entertainment. In writing about creativity as an essential tool for discipleship, Len Wilson notes:

> The work of creative imagination, communicated through story and metaphor, presents a known quantity in a new way, inviting connection and comparison. It unsettles our expectations and causes us to re-evaluate things we may have thought we understood. It seeds growth by raising questions. Jesus was more interested in raising questions than answering them.[3]

Jesus told parables and used object lessons to take something that you already know to tell you something you don't. Stories get people talking. Donald Miller, author of *Building a Storybrand,* cites the science behind why storytelling is so powerful for prompting a response:

> Try singing "Twinkle, Twinkle, Little Star"—without singing the final note on the word "are." It will bother you to no end. That's because your brain is hard-wired to pay attention to what we call "open loops." It's called the Zeigarnik effect, and the idea is that we pay closer attention to those things which aren't completed. Quite simply, our brain holds onto them, waiting for a resolution.[4]

In storytelling terms, this is why we have to stay up late when we start a film to find out who the murderer is behind the mask, whether the couple ends up together, or if the hero will ever get his revenge. The same process occurs even when we have seen the movie before. We already know the ending, but we have to watch the process unfold again and again in order to keep the loop closed. By talking about our experience of Christ, we leave people wanting to know more. Let others long to close the story loop. Create a spiritual itch. Leave spiritual breadcrumbs.

So often, we think that to be successful means we need to reach a vast audience with our creative expressions, but this is simply not the case. In 2016, a group of young adults from a Christian organization called Hope Together started an experimental digital project called "The Gabriel Collective." Their aim was to resource, equip, and network an online group of digital storytellers to share with their peers their everyday life, their faith, and the difference following Jesus makes. They achieved this by encouraging young adults to use *vlogging* to reach their friends around them by sharing their own story.

What was so fascinating is that they were trying to teach people not to use social media to go viral but to go local. It doesn't matter how many people watch it; it matters who watches it. Proximity and locality through reaching *micro-audiences* means two things. First, we're more likely to look like the people we're trying to reach out to. Representation matters. Second, going local means you are more likely to live near the people you're reaching out to. Relationships matter.

What if it's time to release content creators who are local, relatable, representative, and who can engage their own micro-audiences with the power of their story? The more these positive messages of the kingdom are shared in culture—whether encapsulated in stories, songs, poetry, or even billboards—the more we can help prepare the way for Jesus.

REFLECT ═══════════════════════════════════════

Make a list of your own creative gifts and talents, no matter how small.

- *How might you use them to connect people with Jesus?*

- *How could you use a commonly recognized story, symbol, or signifier from creative culture to spark a spiritual conversation?*

14

Hosting

Offer hospitality to one another without grumbling.

1 Peter 4:9

All the best conversations take place when people feel at home.

Ed Debevic's is known as Chicago's most famous retro-themed diner. What makes the 1950s throwback experience so unique is not the taste of the burgers, cheese fries, or jumbo hot dogs (although they are great), it's the way the flashily costumed servers treat the diners. Their website offers this warning: "Don't expect this diner to be a 'Please' and 'Thank You' kind of place, or you might just get your feelings hurt!" (https://www.eddebevics.com). They pride themselves in delivering their food with a side order of what they call "snarky sass."

Our Chicago friends took us there for an evening, and when we arrived, I noticed the funny sign on the front of the diner that says, "Eat and get out!" Inside, the wait staff regularly stopped what they were doing to break out in song, dance, and do anything but pay attention to what they were supposed to be doing. They are known to intentionally deliver the wrong food, make guests visit the kitchen to order their own dessert, and force people to wash up before they can leave.

While this level of over-dramatized intentional unwelcome is hilarious for a night out, no one would want to be treated like that every day! Although the staff at Ed Debevic's are intentionally unwelcoming, as Christians, we are called to deliberately act with the opposite spirit.

Hospitality is about meeting people where they are, at their point of need. It's often inconvenient, disruptive, and it always costs the giver something. Hence, in his letters, Peter encourages us not to moan when we are doing it.

When I visited a Christian conference in Guatemala, I was deeply impacted by the hospitality of strangers. The organizers arranged for a couple to look after us during our stay, and they literally went above and beyond to make sure they did. Afterwards, I wrote about my experience by posting a picture of them and saying:

> This incredible couple has hosted us all week in Guatemala. They have taken time out of their busy schedules to serve us, look after us, pray for us, inspire us, and treat us like VIPs. They didn't know us before we came and have sacrificed with no expectation and obligation. Hospitality is a powerful gift—it enables the people being hosted to be free to receive both from God and people. It shows the love of Christ in such a practical way and in the wonder of the kingdom of God, it somehow leaves everyone richer for the experience.

This idea about treating strangers like VIPs hits right at the heart of what hospitality is all about. When offered from the overflow of a life following Jesus, it blesses both the one who receives and the one who gives. Nothing quite creates the space for conversation to flow like hospitality.

Loving from Our Hearts

Sometimes our drive to reach people for Jesus can ironically cloud our ability to love them well. This shows itself when we use tactics in our hospitality like bait and switch, love bombing, and virtue signaling instead of operating from a Christlike attitude.

Bait and switch. This is where serving others is just an excuse to force our ideas on people without consent. Our motive for meeting practical, emotional, or even social needs is essentially a deceptive marketing ploy. We don't really care about the person other than seeing them as a target for church membership. This can look like inviting a visitor to our house for food, but then tricking them into sitting through a heavy evangelistic rant from us that they never signed up for. When we use bait-and-switch tactics, at best we're not being caring or careful; and at worst, we're actively deceiving people. This is not biblical hospitality.

Love bombing. This is where we attempt to influence a person using attention, affection, and hospitality as a tactic rather than a tool of genuine care. It might look like investing an unsustainable level of time, breaking down personal boundaries too quickly, and excessive flattery. Love bombing can be effective with those who are going through a vulnerable time or are in crisis when they lack confidence and self-esteem. The fine line between this and a healthy, loving kind of care is the motivation behind this behavior. Are we genuine or do we desire only to gain a recruit? We need to be careful that we don't go over the top while they're deciding to be *in* and then drop them once they sign on the dotted line. This isn't ministry. It's manipulation.

Virtue signaling. This is where our good works are used to make us look good. Back in the day, Jesus called out the Pharisees who loved to play out their good deeds in public rather than private. Today, the rise of social media has brought into sharp focus the attempts we make to prove to others that we're good people, but this is only a new manifestation of an ancient problem called pride. Nowadays, we love to tell others about how caring we are (much more than those *other* people) to get likes, hearts, and comments online. This looks like the so-called social influencers who take a selfie of themselves hosting someone, especially someone vulnerable, and post it with the hashtag #blessedtobeablessing.

When we mix our own desires for personal success or looking good into our service for God, we make it more about us than the people we're trying to serve. Self-centeredness, self-validation, and self-sufficiency are all attitudes of *self* that imply that we see ourselves as the heroes of the story and not Jesus. When we focus on what we can do in our own strength, we become the rescuers, not God. Some serve and care for others to feel better about themselves, or they try to earn their way through good works as some form of penance. They get an unhealthy kick from caring that either makes them a martyr or a Martha. But if we act like we don't need Jesus, then we shouldn't expect others to need him either!

These approaches all fly in the face of 1 Corinthians 13, which describes the way of love, and true motivation, as a *love filter* that God intends his people to embrace and model:

> Love never gives up.
> Love cares more for others than for self.
> Love doesn't want what it doesn't have.
> Love doesn't strut,
> Doesn't have a swelled head,
> Doesn't force itself on others,
> Isn't always "me first." (1 Cor. 13:3–7 MSG)

God's command to "love your neighbor" is absolutely vital to being able to fulfill the Great Commission. When we root our actions in love with God and people at the center, we create a firm foundation to help people take their first steps toward Jesus.

Loving from Our Homes

Hospitality is a core value for our family. It is not about the number of resources you have, but about adopting a heart of welcome.

After my wife and I had a lot of input into the early stages of a friend's faith journey, there became an obvious need for her and her young daughter to move out of a difficult home situation. Not wanting them to become disconnected from community, we invited them to come and stay with us. My wife and I were only six months into our marriage, and we didn't really have enough space to make it work, but we figured out how to turn our living room into an extra bedroom. Although we lost a bit of space, we gained a family. The time they spent with us shaped all of our lives.

Nowadays, we are blessed with a bigger house, but that spirit of hospitality lives on. In our home, there is often the sound of teenagers crowding upstairs with music blaring and laughter ringing out of the bedrooms. Then there's the young boy from two doors down who spends so much time in our house he knows exactly where the snack drawer is and can feel free to help himself to it. We are big fans of him. Or the older lady, a retired National Health Service nurse who used to live in Afghanistan, who loves to sit around our table sipping tea and telling stories she's never shared with anyone else. I'm convinced that more cups of tea are drunk in our house than in any other house in Britain! Being hospitable is one of the most impactful ways we still influence others.

Here's what hospitality does for us in all its beauty and simplicity:

- It shows people we love them.
- It allows us the privilege of practically serving others.
- It models something to those around us.
- It becomes a place where joy and laughter break down barriers.
- It quickly builds trust.
- It unlocks gratitude.
- It creates the space for conversation to flow freely.
- It fosters new ideas, perspectives, and stories.
- It's good for you as well as the other person.
- It's a vehicle for discipleship journeys to start, grow, and develop.

The table can encourage a powerful, long meal with laughter and deep life-transforming chats with friends—or strangers who rarely stay that way. This is bigger than just "having people around for a meal." It's a mentality of letting them into *your* world. The writer Terrie Chappell, author of *Heartfelt Hospitality*, speaks about the benefits of having people around our table:

Sitting across the table from someone, listening to blessings and burdens, and sharing Scripture together—these little moments in your home give opportunities to share fellowship and influence others for Christ. As you give of your time and energy to share your home and your heart, God will allow your opportunities to impact others for Him to grow.[1]

At this point, some of you reading this may be feeling anxious or overwhelmed because you don't think your home isn't big or nice enough, your culinary skills aren't good enough, or you're not social enough. Whatever your personality type, hospitality doesn't have to look like something out of a magazine, some picture-perfect ideal. Your home doesn't have to be beautiful; it just has to be open. Whether you offer something big or small, it just has to come from a loving motive.

To help us put hospitality into practice in our everyday lives, church leaders Dave and Jon Ferguson have developed five straightforward practices that can enable us to affect our neighborhoods, whether we're introverts or extroverts. The BLESS model[2] is now used by churches all over the world as a simple tool to help untether the idea of evangelism from the shackles of professionalism, and it encourages everyone in the church to love their neighbors right where they are.

The five steps of the BLESS acronym are:

1. Begin with prayer: Always take time to ask God how he wants us to bless the people we are closest to in our daily lives.

2. Listen with care: Enter the pain, struggles, and challenges of those you walk with.

3. Eat together: Build relationship by eating and drinking together from a place of trust.

4. Serve in love: Figure out what people need so you can serve them well.

5. Share the story: Share your own story about Jesus when the time is right.

We can do all this blessing from the comfort of our own home. These steps feel to me more like rhythms than rules. Each one is a fantastic way to connect others with Jesus.

Loving from Our Community

In *The Celtic Way of Evangelism*,[3] George Hunter explains how the Celtic monks placed hospitality right at the heart of how they sought to influence their world. They made anyone who was spiritually curious or seeking enlightenment feel included before they expected them to meet any criteria for beliefs or behavior. Food was at the heart of this approach. Not only does food bond people together, but hospitality invites people to belong. The monks had a belief that every meal can be a form of ministry.

The Celts who built life together invited others to become part of that community. This is what inspired the popular mantra "Belonging before you believe." This challenges the traditional model of gospel presentation and response followed by integration. Hospitality invites people to assimilate into the Christian community even before they hear about the gospel.

As we consider this Celtic approach, we have to ask if there's space for "belonging" before "believing" in our churches, or if we still expect people to go all in before they're accepted and loved. Do we treat people as targets or tick boxes, or do we honor them as fellow travelers on their own journey toward knowing Jesus?

Since my visit to the picturesque Lindisfarne, known as Holy Island, in Northumberland off the northeast coast of England, I have become even more interested in Celtic history. Once, I traveled with my American friend David Bowden (yes, I know we have a similar name, but that's another story!) to the island, walking to it following the "Pilgrims Way," which is a path across the tidal plain with large wooden posts sticking out of the sand. Over a thousand years earlier, the monks used this same path to walk side by side with people with whom they shared the gospel as they traveled. Holy Island is known as a "thin place"—called so because so many people feel that heaven feels closer to earth here. Some attribute this to the centuries of worship that have taken place on the island. Whatever the reason, it's one of my favorite places in the world.

Part of my motivation to first visit Holy Island was born out of a desire to find out more about one of my new spiritual heroes, Saint Aidan. In AD 635, this monk chose to found his influential monastery on the island. His inspiring approach to spreading the gospel was rooted in both hospitality and pre-discipleship. He was apparently a master at adapting the message of Jesus for the emerging context he found himself in. As one historical commentary notes:

> An inspired missionary, Aidan would walk from one village to another, politely conversing with the people he saw and slowly interesting them in Christianity: in this, he followed the early apostolic model of conversion, by offering "them first the milk of gentle doctrine, to bring them by degrees, while nourishing them with the Divine Word, to the true understanding and practice of the more advanced precepts."[4]

Saint Aidan was not afraid to receive hospitality as well as offer it. Because of this, he patiently led people on their own forms of pilgrimage and transformed the whole of Britain with the gospel.

Loving from Our Churches

When the coronavirus pandemic hit hard in the UK, many churches had to close their doors to meetings in their worshiping community on a Sunday for the first time in over a thousand years. While Sunday services were not possible and the focus moved online, it was apparent across the nation that the vulnerable around us needed more support than ever.

As a response to the crisis, like many others, a group from Mosaic Church in Coventry, where I was formerly the lead pastor, operated the Hope Centre throughout the pandemic and served people in need every single week day for well over a year. To give you a picture of the scale of need, between January and the end of October in 2020, the church fed 5,282 adults and over 3,000 children. This was more than double the adults and three times the number of children they supported during the same period in 2019. The foodbank went from being open for one morning to five mornings a week. For an average-sized church, this effort was nothing short of extraordinary. They went out of their way to keep hospitality at the heart of all they did—even when it became inconvenient to do so.

Yet it wasn't just food they offered. The small, tightly knit team showed how to meet both practical and spiritual needs without the two ever becoming mutually exclusive. This was because they knew why they were doing what they were doing and who they were doing it for. Here is what their hospitality looked like in action:

- They offered an unconditional welcome and positive regard to all.

- They offered practical support, often signposting to other practical services no matter who the person was or where they came from.

- They offered a listening ear and exchanged stories of hope.

- They offered prayer where appropriate (never forced, always with consent).

- They texted messages of hope in the week to stay connected.

- They created support groups for those that had specific life-controlling issues that came up during the lockdown.

- They offered a chance to meet again for those who wanted community.

- They performed funny videos, which went viral online, to keep the City of Coventry smiling.

None of this was done with any sense of a hidden agenda. It was Christians serving with one another for the benefit of those in need. They welcomed strangers as friends, regardless of who they were. They created a sense of community and invited new people in. There was a ruthless focus on the individual (stopping for "the one") and not getting so caught up in serving that they forgot the person being helped. They also invited those who wanted to give back to take part in serving *with* them, even if they weren't Christian. If people came into a toxic, stress-filled, or pressurized environment, then they wouldn't want to stay very long. But when you work together and say, "Hey, we are Christians, and we are here to help"—whatever that help looks like—it can massively impact people in mind, body, and spirit.

Our typical pathways put serving as the pinnacle of belonging, yet in some sense, God has a way of reversing the flow. Having experiences of giving, serving, and loving alongside Christians before someone comes to Christ can actually be a means of inviting them to encounter Jesus. I know so many volunteers in Mosaic Church who have come to Christ through the door of wanting to serve charitably and give something back. What does it look like to laugh, love, and even serve with others *before* they come to Christ? Is this an untapped way to connect more people with Jesus?

What is interesting about this story of the Hope Centre during the pandemic is how the demand for next steps came from those who experienced this loving welcome and asked, "How can we find out more?" First, we opened our doors, and then they opened their hearts. There was no bait and switch; it was "come and see."

People wanted to keep connected because they simply loved being around the volunteers and in the building. Off the back of the food provision came Friday Focus, which was started as soon as in-person gathering was allowed again under the ever-changing government guidelines. Friday Focus was a church meeting for people who had never been to a church meeting. Held late on a Friday afternoon, rather than a Sunday, it comprised 85 percent of those who had no prior experience of church but longed for a taste of community and Christ. It has been a resounding success ever since and is still a veritable disciple-making machine.

Whether from our home, our hearts, or from our churches, serving others in need and offering a warm welcome to all reflects the very heart of God in a tangible way to those around us. So, put out your welcome mat, leave the porch light on, lay out the table (no matter what you have to put on it), and open your life to others. This is a great way for discipleship journeys to begin.

After all, Jesus is the one who first laid out a table for us.

REFLECT

- *What is stopping you, if anything, from showing hospitality to others?*

- *How might you open your heart, your home, or your church more to those around you?*

15

TEACHING

*The things you have heard me say in the presence
of many witnesses entrust to reliable people who
will also be qualified to teach others.*

2 Timothy 2:2

The day my daughter Nyah turned seventeen, I wanted to hide under the sofa because I knew what was about to happen. After the traditional birthday breakfast was out of the way, she sidled up to me with a grin on her face and declared the words I had been dreading to hear: "Now you can teach me to drive!"

Driving lessons with Nyah were like a mixture of a comedy show, a rollercoaster ride, and a horror movie. My wise friends would ask me what time we were going out that week so they could stay off the road. I said my last goodbyes to my wife every time we went for a drive! After the fifteenth near-death experience, both of us were at the end of our tether. Hand brakes had been pulled. Relationships had been stretched.

How do you be someone's dad and their driving instructor at the same time? The solution was to come up with a pact. So I informed Nyah, "I am happy to teach you, but we need to leave our relationship at the door." I became Mr. Boden, and she became my student. This was the only tactic that got us through.

While this approach might work on the road, it doesn't work for people's faith journeys! We can't afford to leave our relationships at the door when it comes to teaching in the church. In fact, most biblical teaching is supposed to happen *through* relationships, not in spite of them. Embedded in the middle of the Great Commission is the phrase, "Teach them to obey." Yet, when we unpack our current teaching models, they often reveal how much they can work against the goal of discipleship and not for it.

Learning happens best within trusting relationships. From the day we are born, a baby sees its mother's face. Our brains are hard-wired to seek positive attachments with other humans. The time when we speed up our spiritual growth at the fastest pace is often when we're surrounded by those who love us.

Often, better learning takes place in a community as opposed to in isolation. It's not just that we learn best *with* others, but we learn best *from* others. When a child learns a new behavior by imitation, they repeat it if it rewards them. One-off actions then become habits as the power of role modeling kicks in. This is why parents who are annoyed at their child's overuse of digital tech ought to check their own usage first. We are natural-born copycats.

While formal teaching settings are great for content impartation, it's life-on-life interactions that lead to deeper character formation. This can't really happen remotely—only through spending time together, eating together, working alongside one another, and deepening our bonds through building trust and connection. Discipleship is always better side by side than row on row.

In our modern church context, we overwhelmingly focus most of our teaching strategy on front-led preaching from the pulpit. Now let me say that I believe wholeheartedly in the power of preaching as a means of God's Spirit touching hearts and changing lives. God can take the feeble imperfect words of a human and anoint them for his glory. But if I add up all the hours of talks that I've listened to over the years, you might expect them to have been more impactful on my day-to-day life than they actually were. Maybe it's just me, but I sometimes struggle to remember what I heard in a church meeting six weeks ago let alone six years!

How many times have we come out of a Sunday meeting feeling good but not feeling changed?

I've sometimes wondered what it would be like if I asked one of the school inspectors I work with to judge an average preaching session from a purely educational perspective. If we had insight into the notes they made during their lesson observation, it might look something like this:

Subject: Rev. Preacher
Sunday Morning Session
Class size: 250
Comments:

> › *The speaker talked nonstop for over thirty minutes with no interaction.*

> › *This was a one-way conversation where rows of passive students faced the active teacher at the front.*

> › *The message was mostly suited to those learners who respond well to auditory, not visual or kinesthetic styles of learning.*

> › *There was no feedback loop, check backs, reflective time, or chance to ask questions.*

> › *The message assumed prior knowledge of the subject and did not differentiate for the needs of all learners.*

> › *It was unclear whether the speaker had personal experience or expertise in the practical application of the subject.*

> › *There was no clear call to action beyond "come down to the front for prayer now." This meant that only 10 percent of the learners knew what to do as a response.*

Judgment: Requires improvement

Okay, this may seem like a harsh caricature of a poor Sunday talk, but it makes a point. Whether or not this is a fair assessment, it's a reminder that overreliance on this style of teaching can sometimes produce passive consumers rather than engaged apprentices.

In their fascinating book *Pagan Christianity*, Frank Viola and George Barna point out that there is often a lack of practical value in our modern obsession with sermonizing everything: "The sermon fails to put the hearers into a direct, practical experience of what has been preached. Thus the typical sermon is a swimming lesson on dry land!"[1]

If we're honest, we're probably over-reliant on Sunday preaching for our spiritual growth. The problem with this is that there's a huge scope for passivity in the learners, and a potential for a lack of accountability when putting that learning into practice. Preaching also has another major stumbling block in that you either need to be in the room to hear it or be willing to listen to a forty-five-minute talk online afterwards.

If it's hard for Christians to grow under this paradigm as the primary means of discipleship, then it's virtually impossible for those not part of the church to connect with it while they're still in the exploration stage of their faith. There are simply too many barriers to entry, whether language, location, or lifestyle.

Teaching versus Learning

There's a difference between *teaching* and *learning*. Our modern word for *teaching* comes from the Old English word *tǣcan*, which means "to show" or "point out." Being a teacher means being a signpost. It's simply imparting knowledge and instruction to others. People can teach with their words and their actions in both formal and informal ways.

Learning is about the addition of new knowledge, skills, values, and behaviors. Learning happens all the time, whether consciously or unconsciously. You don't even need to be taught to learn. One of the interesting tips I picked up from a qualified school teacher is that whenever you're observing a lesson, you shouldn't always look at the teacher at the front but at the students in the class. Their words of advice still resonate with me today: "Just because the teacher is engaged doesn't mean the students are."

Our churches are full of so much teaching. We have pastors who preach their hearts out, and practical programs that fill our calendars. Yet with so much teaching happening, we need to ask: What level of learning is really going on?

I honestly think our approach to knowledge and information would change overnight if we introduced two new rules in church life:

> RULE No. 1: *Learning must be put into practice in our real lives.*
>
> When I signed up for my first skiing lesson before a trip to France, I paid close attention to what I was being taught. I hung on every word the instructor said. Why? Because I knew my life would soon depend on it when I was out on the snowy slopes. This is discipleship: learning as if our life depended on it.
>
> RULE No. 2: *We must all take responsibility to pass on our learning to others.*
>
> If I said that you had to teach someone tomorrow what you're going to learn today, it would make you listen differently. When we have to take responsibility for helping others grow in Christ, it automatically takes our own relationship with Christ to a new level. We were created to learn, to do, and to pass on.

These two rules make us realize that discipleship is never passive, casual, or accidental, even when it's informal. Everyone is passing on something on, but it's our decision to become intentional about it. Discipleship is about learning that leads to lifestyle change with Christlikeness as a goal.

Teaching beyond Preaching

When we see beyond the preaching paradigm that's limited to the few, we can see that teaching can be the activity of the many. Teaching is not just the responsibility of church leaders who have the power to change programs. It's about all of us taking more responsibility for making disciples in our everyday lives. We can teach in so many more ways than we think we can.

- We can teach through conversations.

- We can teach through one-to-one coaching or mentoring.

- We can teach around the dinner table.

- We can teach through creating videos, podcasts, and blogs.

- We can teach through sharing curated resources like books, journals, and magazines.

- We can teach through social media and discussions in our online communities.

- We can teach through modeling spiritual disciplines like praying, giving, and serving.

There are countless ways we can influence spiritual formation, even if we're not on a stage on a Sunday.

Teaching Like Jesus

On one of the last nights on the international school trip to Zambia I mentioned earlier in the book, we took the students out to lie under the stars in the middle of a field. As part of the risk assessment, we had to brush the surrounding ground with brooms to keep any snakes away (I kid you not). Despite the slight fear of reptiles slithering near you, there's no experience like staring at the pitch-black depth and richness of the galaxies in the Southern Hemisphere, away from the bright lights of a city. Lying there in silence, many students shed a tear just thinking about the vastness of the world and their place in it.

Afterwards, we went back inside and watched Pastor Louie Giglio's *Indescribable Tour*,[2] which unpacks the wonders of the known universe to reveal who God is. That night, the conversation flowed about life, faith, and everything in between because of a powerful encounter that engaged all their senses. To this day, I still talk about that night. It was the perfect combination of content curated in creation—and it was our attempt to be a little more Jesus-like in our approach to experiential learning.

Jesus was a master of both reaching and teaching people. Here is a reminder of how he did it and how we can too:

- *Jesus took people outside.* When Jesus taught people on location, whether by a fountain, outside the temple, or on a mountainside, it made learning come alive. He used landscapes to make a point about their Creator. Journeys always became significant whenever Jesus led the way.

- *Jesus used object lessons.* Whether pointing to a tree, a seed, a lampstand, or a patch of soil, Jesus used the power of "see it and speak it" to engage learners. For those at the "not interested" end of the Engel Scale, object lessons act as a fantastic learning hook. When you start with something instantly recognizable to someone and then invite them to consider a new perspective, it's almost like a preview or trailer that stimulates interest.

- *Jesus told stories.* Talking about judges, shepherds, or widows made learning stick. Subverting stereotypes was key to making this kind of message so powerful. You expect someone to behave in a certain way and then become confused when the rug is pulled out from under you. Why did the judge show mercy? Why did the father run down the road? The best stories build on prior learning as a springboard for introducing something new or unexpected.

- *Jesus led people in an experience of spiritual disciplines.* Rather than just teach about a subject, Jesus immediately called people to action. There is growing evidence that helping people experience spiritual disciplines like prayer, meditation, and even social action can act as a tool to connect them with God, even if they don't have a prior connection with faith. The expectation was that people could model what Jesus was talking about in their own time and in their own way. "When you pray, pray like this. . . "

- *Jesus engaged in conversation around the table.* So many of the formative moments in the disciples' journey took place around eating. Information, knowledge, wisdom, and insight were often shared around the table rather than from a stage or platform. He encouraged group discussion and participation among peers. This two-way interaction helped strengthen beliefs, embody values, and draw long-lasting conclusions. There is something powerful about pizza and proximity.

- *Jesus gave real-world instructions.* Like an excellent teacher, Jesus observed his students as they applied learning. As he sent out his disciples to heal the sick and preach the gospel, they learned by doing, engaging with opportunities to practice and test knowledge. Jesus even made sure they came back for further instruction and check backs. On-the-job learning is always better!

- *Jesus role-modeled what he taught.* Everywhere Jesus went, he embodied his message. There was no lack of integrity between what he said and did daily. His life was his lesson. This is quite a challenge for us!

Jesus' three-dimensional approach to teaching is so powerful when we think about how we can reach and teach people in our everyday lives. All of these tools can be used as we walk alongside people. Every one of us can be a teacher. Why? Because we have *the* great teacher with us, and we have his word to guide us. The word of God is dynamite for discipleship.

REFLECT ══════════════════════════════════════

As you consider how Jesus taught others, what are some ways you can incorporate his style of teaching into how you share your knowledge, skills, and values with those with whom you are walking?

16

UNPACKING

*Do your best to present yourself to God as one
approved, a worker who does not need to be ashamed
and who correctly handles the word of truth.*

2 Timothy 2:15

In the famous courtroom scene at the end of *A Few Good Men*, we
see military lawyer Lieutenant Daniel Kaffee, brilliantly played
by Tom Cruise, go up against Colonel Jessup, depicted by the
inimitable Jack Nicholson, as he defends a Marine accused of
murder. For anyone who has seen the film, you can literally hear
the harsh tone of their voices and feel the electricity between
them when you read the tense exchange below.

> LT. KAFFEE: Colonel Jessup, did you order the Code Red?
>
> JUDGE RANDOLPH: You don't have to answer that question.
>
> COL. JESSUP: I'll answer the question. You want answers?
>
> LT. KAFFEE: I think I'm entitled to them.
>
> COL. JESSUP: You want answers?!
>
> LT. KAFFEE: I want the truth!
>
> COL. JESSUP: *You can't handle the truth!*

Handling the truth is not just for the courtrooms but for the
living rooms of those we are walking alongside. The term "correctly handle" in 2 Timothy originates from the concept of "cutting

a straight line." Some people think Paul may have been using an expression that tied in with his trade as a tentmaker. Back in the day, they made tents from the skins of animals in a patchwork sort of design, and every piece had to be fitted together as part of a bigger pattern. If one didn't cut the pieces right, then the whole thing might not fit together properly. Perhaps this was the essence of Paul's charge to Timothy regarding the Scriptures? The Bible is not a textbook just to be studied; it's a living and active tool for spiritual formation.

When we're walking side by side with someone, we can't just default to business mantras, pithy sayings, lifestyle hacks, and top tips. Ultimately, we have to find ways of appropriately sharing Bible verses, passages, moments, and stories that are key to bringing lasting change. If there's no engagement with the Bible, then there's no chance of long-term transformation into the likeness of Christ.

Before someone decides to follow Christ, we should start to include references to Scripture in our conversations and our connections with them in ways, such as:

- Tell a story about Jesus.
- Find an answer to a question.
- Illustrate a point of conversation.
- Bring comfort or even conviction.
- Share about our own response to the Bible.

Then, over time, there could be a more formal approach, a habit, a regular engagement, or even a study. Or it may stay as an informal flow. That's okay. There's no one-size-fits-all. Everything moves at the speed of trust.

Minding the Gap

The call to correctly handle the word of God still stands for us today. Yet over two thousand years later, there are new challenges we need to overcome that even Timothy didn't have to contend with.

First, there is an issue about Scripture among Christians.

Bible disengagement is growing. The 2022 State of the Bible report[1] from the American Bible Society highlights an unprecedented drop in the percentage of Bible users in the United States. Their *Bible disengagement* category grew by almost 40 percent in one year. Engagement is falling off a cliff.

Bible relevance is waning. When we look at social media, we see the Bible used to clobber people with proof-texts. Or we position it as another self-soothing set of self-help quotes and sayings to help us feel better as we look at the internet and drink coffee. We have given the Bible a bad name by making it too harsh or too soft.

Second, there's a challenge of the perception of non-Christians.

The Bible is often seen as an ancient book that has been over-edited, copied incorrectly, and is full of contradictions. People have huge misconceptions and myths about what the Bible might say, let alone have problems with what it actually says. Many think all religious texts are the same and that the stories in Scripture are just borrowed from ancient cultures. All in all, there are many issues that confront those who may not be quick to respond when you try to talk about what "the Bible says."

As a new generation becomes curious about Christ, they will inevitably need to tackle the Bible, and we should be equipped to walk with them as they do. We need to "mind the gaps" as we seek to understand Scripture. Which gaps are we talking about?

- Time gaps
- Geographical gaps
- Cultural gaps
- Language gaps
- Writing gaps
- Supernatural gaps

Considering these gaps, we need to handle Scripture with care. Many Christians vary wildly in their conservative or liberal views—with both sides throwing around the phrase "the Bible says" while often misunderstanding the basics of how to actually interpret it.

We all interpret the Bible. The question is, Do we interpret it responsibly?

While I won't advocate for a left or right position here, you can guarantee that others will ask you some fairly comprehensive and even challenging questions about the word of God when you get deeper with people, so you need to unpack it for yourself.

Mark Twain famously said, "It ain't those parts of the Bible that I can't understand that bother me; it is the parts that I do understand."

We have to develop the skills that will help us get to grips with the Bible so that we can apply it to our life. Knowing how to engage with the Bible will also help you serve others. This starts by gaining a bird's-eye view. You can't answer every tricky question, nor do you always need to, but there are some basic approaches that will help you line up your ducks.

The Tools of the Truth

The point of this chapter is to help frame how you might approach tackling the Bible in a culture that can often be hostile, disinterested, or even vitriolic toward the idea that an ancient book can carry any sense of authority for the modern world. But it is still the world's number one bestselling book. And it is still the divine word of God.

Here are five simple tools to help frame not *what* you read but *how* you read the Bible with those with whom you are walking. Each of these will help provide a foundation to tackle some of the objections that are bound to come, whatever they may be.

Tool 1: Classification

We need to help those we walk alongside see that the Bible needs to be classified according to genre.

On Sunday, October 30, 1938, the United States experienced a big problem caused by incorrect classification. When Orson Welles performed a realistic radio broadcast of H. G. Wells' *War of the Worlds*, people mistakenly believed it was an authentic news report, causing mass panic and fear of an alien invasion. It was a serious case of mistaken genre.

The Bible is not one book but a library of books, so we need to identify which kind of literature we're reading to help us understand it. That's classification. Each genre communicates in a unique style or structure. You read a science textbook differently than you read a novel, just as you read a newspaper differently than an email from a friend. What's the genre of the book you're currently reading? Is it narrative, law, prophecy, poetry, history, or a letter? This impacts how we understand it.

Should we read the Bible literally? It depends on which genre you're dealing with. We need to look carefully at the language of the text within the genre. Is the passage using metaphors or other figures of speech such as hyperbole (deliberate exaggeration)? How does this affect the overall meaning of the passage? We can assume that each word in a passage has a normal, literal meaning, unless there is good reason to view it as a figure of speech. If you're not sure, how might you find out more?

We need to read the Bible *literarily* as much as we read it literally!

Tool 2: Context

We need to help those we walk alongside see that context matters in the Bible.

The Bible clearly says that there is no God! It's right there in Psalm 14:1. Look it up: "There is no God." Obviously, I'm conveniently overlooking how those words are introduced: "The fool says in his heart, 'There is no God.'"

The context in which any passage is written influences how it is to be understood. Some scholars reckon we could probably answer two-thirds of questions about the meaning of any Bible passage just by reading the complete text.

We don't need to overcomplicate it. People jump through hoops to make a passage mean what they want it to mean. I have even seen people deliberately stay in confusion, ignorance, or intentional blindness so they don't have to respond to the word!

Context includes several things like:

- The verses immediately before and after a passage. This is often where the convenient division of chapter and verse can sometimes be unhelpful, as we are prone to see things in isolation.
- The paragraph and book in which the verses appear.
- The time and culture in which it was written.
- The message and themes of the entire Bible.

Consider if instructions, commands, or blessings in both the Old and New Testament were specific to individual circumstances or can be applied universally to all today. For example, Jesus told his disciples to go into town and find a donkey. Is that for me or just them?

We also need to understand the difference between descriptive and prescriptive in the Bible. For example, you may read a story in the Old or New Testament where a character behaves in a horrific way. We don't have to be confused or offended by this. It's not prescribing how we should respond, or even endorsing the behavior; it's merely relaying it for future generations.

While I was sitting around the dinner table with friends in the church in Sarande, Albania, we awkwardly started trying to tell jokes to one another that none of us really understood. It wasn't the unfamiliar language that got to us; it was the lack of context.

No Albanian could quite figure out why the chicken crossed the road, and why that was supposed to be funny. But every five minutes, one of them would repeat this joke to our group: "You know Georgie? He is from Greece!" That's it. That's the joke. And it's one that sent my Albanian friends rolling in the aisles every time.

Why did we fail to get the gag? Two things: context and culture. We default to see everything through either our twenty-first-century lens or from our own Western perspective.

The Bible was written to address real people who were living in actual locations and times for a genuine reason. When we look into the context more, we can understand what the writers intended the text to mean to their original audience. In doing so, it helps us find meaning for our lives today.

TOOL 3: CHRIST-CENTEREDNESS

We need to help those we walk alongside see that the Bible centers on Jesus.

What's the most powerful page in the Bible? The blank one between the Old and New Testaments. We have to view the whole of Scripture through the lens of the message, life, death, and resurrection of Christ. It's like seeing the original Star Wars trilogy from beginning to end and already knowing the crucial "Luke, I am your father" plot twist. It changes how you see everything that has gone before.

When Jesus encountered two disciples on the road to Emmaus, he taught the greatest Bible study of all time, unveiling the Scriptures through the lens of himself.

> And beginning with Moses and all the Prophets, he explained to them what was said in all the Scriptures concerning himself.
> (Luke 24:27)

We find shadows, types, and precursors of Christ all over Scripture. From Genesis where he is the seed of the woman, to Revelation where he is the Alpha and the Omega. Every page whispers his name. Jesus is the visible image of an invisible God. All conclusions about the nature of God need to be put through the filter of Christ.

There is a great visual example of the supremacy of Christ in the story of the Mount of Transfiguration found in Matthew 17. Alongside Moses (representing the law) and Elijah (representing the prophets), Jesus' true nature is revealed to three of his disciples as a voice from heaven declares that we are to listen to Jesus. The book of Hebrews echoes this when it tells us that in the past God spoke through his prophets, but in the last days God has spoken to us through Jesus.

Where does the passage you're looking at fit in the Jesus story? Not just which chapter of the Bible are you in, but which chapter in history?

Taking a Christ-centered approach to Scripture is like viewing the landscape from the heights of the mountain top and not the depths of the valley. Everything looks different from the right perspective. We don't ignore or diminish the rest of the Bible, but we do need to reframe it.

TOOL 4: CROSS-REFERENCING

We need to help those we walk alongside see that the Bible can speak for itself.

For the past twelve years, there has been one series of films I never fail to see at the cinema with at least one of my children. I love the Marvel Cinematic Universe because it's so connected. Every story arc and character somehow links to the next—from Iron Man to Spider Man and Rocket to Groot. Fans look for clues known as "Easter Eggs" hidden in films to help them gain an understanding of the bigger story.

The idea of an interconnected universe is nothing new—we find it first in the Bible. Many times, the imagery or language in the New Testament mimics or expands that of the Old. When Peter says, "You are a royal priesthood," he is directly referencing passages from Exodus and Deuteronomy. The book of Revelation is full of references to the Old Testament prophetic imagery and can't be understood apart from this interconnectedness.

We need to see all Scripture as part of the Biblical Cinematic Universe.

Let the Bible interpret the Bible. When looking at a topic or theme ask, "Where else does the Bible talk about this?" If you can't figure out a verse, look for comparisons but be careful not to assume that the same word or phrase in two different passages means the same thing. For example, the picture of yeast is symbolic of the kingdom of God, but it's also a picture of false doctrine. It's also sometimes simply referring to actual yeast!

As we read, we see there are big recurring themes that sweep across the whole architecture of Scripture: From creation to new creation.

Tool 5: Consultation

We need to help those we walk alongside see that they can explore the Bible in consultation.

Consult with God. We can always ask the Spirit to help us "open our eyes" and gain divine revelation. It's not just about head knowledge but also heart transformation.

Consult with others. We can get much out of reading together and answering a few key questions such as: What does this passage teach us about the nature of God, or what does it teach us about the nature of people? As you discuss and share your perspective together, it can bring fresh revelation even if the person has yet to declare their trust in Jesus.

Consult with resources. If in doubt, ask for help! Reading books, study guides, and commentaries can help you interpret Scripture more effectively. Many people have done a lot of heavy lifting to help us on our journey. Be prepared to recommend resources and also rhythms that make a difference. You might want to share the following ideas for understanding Scripture with those you're walking alongside.

- *Listen to it.* Listen to an audio version of the Bible as you travel to and from work or go about your business. Download a Bible app such as the YouVersion Bible so you have it on your smartphone. You can even listen on Amazon Alexa.

- *Study it.* Get a study guide or Bible commentary (a book about the Bible) to help you go deeper. These help you answer questions like: "What is the writer trying to communicate?" and "Who is their intended audience?"

- *Journal it.* Write notes in a journal or make notes and drawings in the margins of your Bible to respond as creatively as you want!

- *Read aloud with it.* Faith comes by hearing, so speak it out and see what happens!

- *Pray with it.* Before and after you read, ask God to speak and then be ready to listen. The Bible is inspired by God, so ask the Holy Spirit to help you understand what you read—and make a note of any questions that arise.

- *Engage with others through it.* Reading the Bible with other people opens incredible opportunities to share inspiration as well as explore questions and gain insight from one another.

You can mix and match your approach whether by reading front to back, book by book, chapter by chapter, verse by verse, theme by theme, or character by character. If you get to the point where you're regularly exploring the Bible with someone with whom you're exploring faith, then a good rule of thumb may be to follow this kind of question structure together:

- What are you reading?

- What is God saying to you?

- What are you doing about it?

When the disciples walked with Christ on the road to Emmaus, we see that the truth made a head-to-heart impact on them. Jesus opened their eyes. Their inner passion and drive were transformed. They received a sense of hope, direction, and purpose. They were on fire for Christ. Nothing else can do this in the same way except a fresh revelation from walking with Jesus and his Scriptures.

As the saying goes: "You don't read the Bible. The Bible reads you."

REFLECT ════════════════════════════════════

How do you think the toolkit of truth will help you when you engage in conversations about the Scriptures with:

- *Those who are not yet followers of Jesus?*
- *Those who are followers of Jesus?*

17

BIRTHING

Therefore, if anyone is in Christ, the new creation
has come: The old has gone, the new is here!

2 Corinthians 5:17

Back in the mid-2000s, I attended a large outreach event with a
bunch of teenagers from our neighborhood youth group. Most
had never attended a church meeting in their life before. A well-
known speaker from overseas delivered a rousing message that
was dynamic, enigmatic, and that presented the gospel.

At the end of the message came the time for the appeal. They
asked the young people who wanted to respond to the gospel
to go into a side room while the rest of the audience played a
fun game. So, after some discussion, we split the group with
those who wanted to know more about Jesus and those happy to
have some fun. Once in the side room, they were immediately
asked to fill in a response card with their name, address, and
contact details. This was a challenge for us because we hadn't
got prior permission from their parents to give out this kind of
information.

After some awkward engagement with the organizers, we let
a few fill in some basic details, and the young people were then
sent back to their seats with no other explanation about the decision (or lack thereof) they had just made. There was no space
for conversation, no clarification, or any explanation. It was all
focused around getting the young person, some of whom had just

heard about a loving God for the first time and felt quite moved by the message, to fill in a contact card.

That was it.

Standing at the back of the side room, I watched as an enthusiastic leader counted up the response cards with glee and declared how many people had given their lives to Jesus. While they were busy counting cards, I could see that one young girl clearly wanted to talk with them about what was happening with her but was missed in the moment.

What's interesting is that not a single one of the young people who had filled in a card ever received any kind of follow-up, but I heard about the numerical success of the outreach event in local Christian circles for months.

With Christian outreach, we are very good at the ramp-up and fairly poor at follow-up.

According to some research, on average, a person needs to hear the gospel three times before they respond.[1] This means a decision to commit their whole lives is unlikely to happen the first time they hear about Jesus. What if someone is not quite ready? Then invite them to take another step and trust God with the outcome.

My warm and funny friend, Mark Greenwood, is Elim's National Evangelist for the UK. Having led countless people to faith in Jesus, he understands well the process of what making a healthy decision for Christ looks like:

> If you ever listen to someone telling you their story of how they came to faith in Christ, most people's journey involved them at some point traveling through the "healthy maybe" on their way to a "little yes" and a "big yes." I've met so many people when they've been in the "healthy maybe" stage. It excites me because at this stage they are on the way. If we're not careful, we can put such a big focus on a person committing their life to Christ, we end up not celebrating all the little decisions along the way.[2]

From this process-oriented concept, Mark has trained thousands of people in what he calls the "Big Yes, Little Yes, Healthy Maybe" framework, which he brilliantly applies with care when doing both altar calls and walking with people in everyday life. Here is what each of the three stages means in terms of a next step:

- *Big Yes.* Saying a heartfelt yes to God and becoming a Christian.

- *Little Yes.* Making an intentional decision to look into the Christian faith.

- *Healthy Maybe.* A willingness to become or remain open-minded.[3]

Even if someone is not quite ready for the "big step," they may want to take a small one. This is a great example of shifting pre-discipleship into discipleship mode. Always leave people with a way to make progress and never assume someone else will do it.

Saying Yes to Following Jesus

While the focus of this book has been on helping people take their first steps toward Jesus, I would be remiss if I didn't cover a healthy approach for what to do when someone responds to God and finds themselves in a place where they want to become a Christian.

What happens when a person with whom we're walking doesn't feel manipulated or rushed but is actually asking how they can make a choice? What do we do if we get a resounding "big yes," like the jailor who grabbed Paul and Silas and asked, "What must I do to be saved?"

Usually at this point, we find ourselves either scrambling for our pastor's phone number or googling the "sinner's prayer." But I believe we should empower every follower of Christ to be confident enough to connect anyone with Jesus. It's the most loving thing we can ever do to lead others across to Jesus.

Becoming a Christian is about saying yes to God, but it's also about saying no to yourself. This is what it means to give your life to Jesus. Becoming a disciple is about making a personal decision to live for Jesus, learn with Jesus, love like Jesus, and in doing so, seek to look like Jesus. People need to understand that they're not a Christian just because their parents are, or because they've attended church meetings, or because they were christened as a child, went to a Catholic school, or live in a "Christian" country. A person is a Christian if they've responded to the good news of Jesus and chosen for themselves, without coercion, to surrender their lives to God and live for him every day.

You can't inspire or argue someone into their salvation. If a decision is based purely on an emotional response, then their will to continue may pass with that feeling. Nor can you just logically argue someone into the kingdom of God, lest they become demotivated as soon as a better option or a more logical argument comes along. It takes the submission of our minds, emotions, and wills to cross the line of faith.

This is not our work to do, but a work of God's power alone. Yet as coworkers with him, we have a part to play. There is a three-way partnership going on between the work of the Holy Spirit to convict, the word of God to reveal truth, and the coworker to act as a point of connection.

In his book *Living Proof*, Jim Peterson reminds us to remember our distinct job description:

> It is important to keep this division of labor clear in our minds. For us to attempt to do the work of the Holy Spirit or that of the scriptures is futile. If a person is convinced by the Spirit of God, and spiritually reborn through the word of God, we can be confident of the kind of new life that has been created. It will bear fruit. As for us we have the privilege of making the introductions.[4]

As Paul says in Romans 10:9–10,

> If you declare with your mouth, "Jesus is Lord," and believe in your heart that God raised him from the dead, you will be saved. For it is with your heart that you believe and are justified, and it is with your mouth that you profess your faith and are saved.

According to this verse, for a person to be ready to follow Jesus, they simply need to remember their ABCs:

- Admit that they need Jesus Christ (this is the foundation of repentance).

- Believe what Jesus Christ has done for them through his life, death, and resurrection.

- Confess their faith before God and others.

Leading Someone to Christ

Many of us have seen the enthusiastic preacher stand at the pulpit and at the end of their rousing preach on any topic give an altar call that goes something like:

> How many of you want to say *yes* to Jesus today? I am going to count to three, and then I want you to raise your hand. One . . . two . . . three . . . I see that hand. Praise the Lord! I SEE THAT HAND!

The problem with this type of well-intended appeal is that it makes a lot of presuppositions:

- It assumes that the person knows what they are saying yes to.

- It assumes the person understands the gospel even if it wasn't explicitly shared as part of the meeting.

- It assumes the person will make the deduction that saying yes to God means saying no to living life by their own standards and that they will turn to God in repentance.

I am not at all against so-called altar calls in church meetings, but I think that how we execute them matters. Unless time has been taken before, during, or after the meeting to offer a clear gospel explanation, led by the Holy Spirit, and using language the audience will understand, then the organizers are often in effect are skipping A (admission) and B (belief) and starting at C (confess). This is like asking people to sign on the dotted line without explaining the small print! Any mass invitation should always include consistent and explicit personal follow-up. Otherwise, we risk inoculating people against the effectiveness of the gospel. They might say that they've already responded because they put up their hand once and mistakenly believe this is enough to follow Jesus always.

Praying with others to help them connect with Jesus can happen in any situation, in any place, and not just in a church meeting. Intention is way more important than location. What's important is that we always act out of our love for the person rather than our enthusiasm for the moment.

You don't have to be a priest, a pastor, or a professional to lead a person to Christ. There's no such thing as a "Sinner's Prayer" in the Bible. Any response ought to be rooted in the ABCs above, which interestingly are more about personal reflection and confession than just prayer. However, taking time to pray with anyone who wants us to help them turn their heart toward God is one way of marking a moment of transition. I have a friend who always celebrates two birthdays: the first is the day they were born, and the second marks the day they were born again. This can be a helpful marker for that person to point back to when the going gets tough.

If you're anything like me, then reeling off some rehearsed script or memorized statement is likely to be an issue in the heat of the moment, so I just remember three words that help shape praying with people at their point of decision. I always think about what parents teach their children to say when they're young: thank you, sorry, please!

- *Say thank you.* "Thank you for making me, loving me, and dying for me to bring me back to relationship with you."

- *Say sorry.* "Sorry for messing up and living life on my own agenda and by my own rules."

- *Say please.* "Please come in to my life and save me,
  become the boss of my life, heal me from my past, help
  me to live for you, and be with me every step of the way."

It's far better to pray naturally with the person as opposed to operating from a set script, but you could ask them to repeat a prayer after you if it helps them focus. The point is to be led by the one you are praying for, not by your predetermined ideals.

Doing the Next Right Thing

Taking personal responsibility to be proactive after someone decides to follow Christ will mean the new disciple has the best chance of not falling on the first hurdle. There are, therefore, some practical steps we should take as part of the immediate short-term follow up before the long-term walk begins.

- *Rejoice.* When someone decides to follow Christ,
  celebrate with them (Jesus said that even the angels are
  rejoicing!) and encourage them to share that decision
  with others if it's safe to do so. Don't forget to mark the
  moment with thanksgiving. It helps create an anchor
  point for the future.

- *Reassure.* Whether they felt anything or not at the
  moment they prayed, God saved them and they're now
  part of God's family! Pray a prayer of blessing over their
  life. Answer questions they may have. Bring comfort. Affirm joy. Acknowledge peace.

- *Remind.* Remind them of the next step. Give them something practical to do. This may mean telling them when
  and how they can connect into a local church community, whether one to one or in a small group or meeting.
  It may also be about talking with you again. Put a date in
  the diary. Keep the steps moving.

- *Relate.* Encourage them to pray and connect to God for
  themselves. Share tips on how to do this. Let them enjoy
  the freedom of this new relationship with God from day

one! The Lord's Prayer is a timeless classic for working through a structure for how to pray simply.

- *Read.* Ask the person if they have access to a Bible (physical or online) and set them up to read about the life of Jesus in Matthew, Mark, Luke, or John. Alternatively, they can listen to Scripture online or try a quick study on a Bible app. Ask them to make a note of anything they don't understand to talk later with you about. Share some simple Bible reading tips and tactics that work for you. Feed their faith.

- *Reality check.* Tell them that although they may not overcome all their challenges and problems straight away, God is with them and will walk them through to freedom. This is vital as we are dealing with a spiritual dimension, not just a practical one. Darkness doesn't like light. But there's no need to be afraid. God is with us in both the valley and on the mountaintop!

- *Reconnect.* Check up on the person within a few days. Don't rely on someone else to do this! Pray for them throughout the following week. Make sure they have someone they can connect with and relate to. Introduce them to a church community. It's no longer all about you. Connection is key.

- *Reorient.* Talk to the person about baptism in water when the time is right. Baptism is an outward symbol of an inward transformation. It's a physical act expressing a spiritual truth, a public confession to the world that we identify with the death, burial, and resurrection of Jesus. There are different schools of thought relating to when a person is ready for this to happen. Some church traditions opt for a more considered approach with elements of formal training, while others advocate it should be done as soon as possible. There are also sensitive cultural considerations for some. However you work this out, ensure it's part of your discussion as early as possible.

Although these are the obvious next steps, you'll be amazed at how many times these they're skipped. Follow-up is the key to lasting change.

There is a danger here that we unintentionally present making a concrete decision to follow Christ as the end goal and not the start of the journey for a new believer. Moving beyond the pre-discipleship stage is about helping people see that their decision for Christ is part of the process, not the conclusion of it.

If we have mastered the art of walking side by side with others before they come to Jesus, then there's no reason we can't continue this afterwards. Imagine the day when you see the smile on their face, hear their stories of hope, and watch their life transform before your very eyes! There's literally no better thrill on this side of heaven.

Except for one more joy to come: When you see them start to do the same with others.

But for now, all you have to do is keep on walking!

REFLECT ═══

As you consider the whole of this book,

- *What do you think you need to stop doing?*

- *What do you need to start?*

- *What will you continue?*

Final Prayer

Dear God,

Thank you for the privilege of leading others
one step closer to you.
Help me discern the right time to ask
and the right time to listen.
Give me the words to say.
Grant me the wisdom to gently
guide people toward you.
And let the one I am leading to you be filled with joy.
Let them know your peace.
Guard them from fear and harm.
And may we walk together side by side
until we both fix our eyes on you.

Amen

Notes

Introduction

1. Sharan Faur and Brett Laursen, "Classroom Seat Proximity Predicts Friendship Formation," *Frontiers in Psychology* (May 2022), https://www.frontiersin.org/articles/10.3389/fpsyg.2022.796002/full.

2. Zach Baron, "The Redemption of Justin Bieber," *GQ* (May 2021), https://www.gq.com/story/justin-bieber-cover-profile-may-2021.

3. Alex Murashko, "Study: Churchgoers Say Sharing Faith Essential, Many Never Do," *Christian Post* (August 2012), https://www.christianpost.com/news/study-churchgoers-say-sharing-faith-essential-many-never-do.html.

4. Alan Hirsch, *Disciplism: Reimagining Evangelism through the Lens of Discipleship* (Exponential Resources, 2014), 23.

5. Pete Scazzero, "Why Megachurch Pastors (and Other Leaders) Fail and How to Sustain a Healthy Inner Life," Carey Nieuwhof Leadership Podcast: Episode 438, August 2021.

Chapter 1

1. C. S. Lewis, *Yours, Jack: The Inspirational Letters of C. S. Lewis* (London: HarperCollins UK, 2009), 9.

2. C. S. Lewis, *Collected Letters Volume One: Family Letters 1905–1931* (London: HarperCollins UK, 2000), 970.

3. Tony Morgan, "Why Your Discipleship Path Is More Important Than Ever (and the Strategic Steps That We've Found Work Well)," *The Unstuck Group* (January 2023), https://theunstuckgroup.com/why-your-discipleship-path-is-more-important-than-ever-and-the-strategic-steps-that-weve-found-work-well/.

Chapter 2

1. Barna Group, "Signs of Decline and Hope Among Key Metrics of Faith," *State of the Church Research* (2020), https://www.barna.com/research/changing-state-of-the-church/.

2. Milton Quintanilla, "Almost 70 Percent of Born-Again Christians Say Jesus Christ Isn't the Only Way to God, Study Shows," *Christian Headlines* (October 2021), https://www.christianheadlines.com/contributors/milton-quintanilla/almost-70-percent-of-born-again-christians-say-jesus-christ-isnt-the-only-way-to-god-study-shows.html.

3. Peter Brierley, *UK Church Statistics 2, 2010–2020* (Birmingham, UK: ADBC, 2014).

4. Aaron Earls "Most Teenagers Drop Out of Church When They Become Young Adults," *Lifeway Research* (January 2019), https://research.lifeway.com/2019/01/15/most-teenagers-drop-out-of-church-as-young-adults/.

5. Cris Rogers, *Making Disciples: Elevating the Conversation around Discipleship and Spiritual Formation* (UK: Essential Christian, 2018), 7.

6. Rich Villodas (@richvillodas), Twitter, July 31, 2022, https://twitter.com/richvillodas/status/1553893420019621890.

Chapter 3

1. John Mark Comer, *Live No Lies: Recognize and Resist the Three Enemies That Sabotage Your Peace* (London: SPCK, 2021), 73.

2. Will Mancini and Cory Hartman, *Future Church: Seven Laws of Real Church Growth* (Grand Rapids: Baker Books, 2020), 15.

Chapter 4

1. James Engel and Wilbert Norton, *What's Gone Wrong with the Harvest? Communication Strategy for the Church and World Evangelism* (Grand Rapids: Zondervan, 1975).

2. Engel and Norton, *What's Gone Wrong with the Harvest?*, 45.

3. Tony Morgan, "Multisite Ministry Movement Trends with Tony Morgan," *Vanderbloemen Leadership Podcast*, March 2021, https://www.vanderbloemen.com/blog/multisite-ministry-movement-trends.

4. Laurence Singlehurst, *Faith and Society: Re:focus Sowing Reaping Keeping Training* (Didcot, UK: Baptist Union of Great Britain, 2012), https://www.baptist.org.uk/Articles/366602/Re_focus_Sowing.aspx.

5. Alpha International, *Global Impact Study 2016*, https://alpha.org.uk/global-impact-study.

6. Tony Scialdone, "What Is the Engel Scale?," *GodWords*, 2023, https://godwords.org/what-is-the-engel-scale/.

Chapter 5

1. Kai Mark, *Pre-Discipleship: The Forgotten Element in Evangelism* (Word Alive Press, 2009), loc. 1380, Kindle.

Chapter 6

1. Laura Silver et al., "What Makes Life Meaningful? Views from 17 Advanced Economies," *Pew Research Center*, November 18, 2021, https://www.pewresearch.org/global/2021/11/18/what-makes-life-meaningful-views-from-17-advanced-economies/.

2. Barna Group, "Reviving Evangelism Report" (2019), https://www.barna.com/research/millennial-spiritual-curiosity/.

3. Josiah Venture UK, "Strategy," (2023), https://www.josiahventure.org.uk/about/strategy.

4. Celeste Ng, "Stay Open," in *Radical Hope: Letters of Love and Dissent in Dangerous Times*, ed. Carolina De Robertis (New York: Vintage Books, 2017), 222–26.

5. Darin and Joy Stevens, "How Do We Stir Curiosity?," *Start to Stir* (blog), https://www.starttostir.com/blog/how-to-stir.

Chapter 7

1. Barna Group, "Two in Five Christians Are Not Engaged in Discipleship" (January 2022), https://www.barna.com/research/christians-discipleship-community/.

2. Heidi Baker, *Compelled by Love: How to Change the World through the Simple Power of Love in Action* (Lake Mary, FL: Charisma House, 2008), 35.

3. David Platt, *Radical: Taking Back Your Faith from the American Dream* (Colorado Springs: Multnomah, 2010), 90.

Chapter 8

1. James Clear, "Identity-Based Habits: How to Actually Stick to Your Goals This Year," *James Clear*, https://jamesclear.com/identity-based-habits.

2. James Clear, "3-2-1: On taking action, changing incentives, and belonging," *James Clear*, June 4, 2020, https://jamesclear.com/3-2-1/june-4-2020.

3. "Ambassador," *Collins Dictionary*, https://www.collinsdictionary.com/dictionary/english/ambassador.

4. Jay Pike, "Equipping Christians in Church, Commerce, and Community," Forward Conference UK, March 30, 2019.

Chapter 9

1. Living and Telling, "About," *Campus Crusade for Christ*, https://livingtelling.com/about.shtml.

2. Jim Petersen, *Living Proof: Sharing the Gospel Naturally* (Colorado Springs: NavPress, 1989), 96.

3. #LifeOnMisson, "How to Make Jesus Interesting When Cat Videos Exist" (@YesHEis), Instagram, April 2022, https://www.instagram.com/p/CcNi98oo31q/?igshid=YmMyMTA2M2Y=.

Chapter 10

1. Jill Suttie, "How Smartphones are Killing Conversation," *Greater Good Magazine* (December 2015), https://greatergood.berkeley.edu/article/item/how_smartphones_are_killing_conversation.

2. Susannah Newsonen, "When Did We Stop Talking to Each Other?," *Psychology Today* (February 2018), https://www.psychologytoday.com/us/blog/the-path-passionate-happiness/201802/when-did-we-stop-talking-each-other.

Chapter 11

1. David Foster Wallace, "This Is Water," *James Clear*, https://jamesclear.com/great-speeches/this-is-water-by-david-foster-wallace.

2. Wallace, "This Is Water."

3. Julian Rappaport, Community Narratives: Tales of Terror and Joy," *American Journal of Community Psychology* 28 (February 2000): 1–24, https://doi.org/10.1023/A:1005161528817.

4. John Mark Comer, "CNLP 440: John Mark Comer on Why We Believe Lies about Freedom, Sex, Truth and Culture, How the Left and the Right Fail, and the Way Forward for the Church," Carey Nieuwhof Leadership Podcast Episode 440, September 2021, https://podcasts.apple.com/gb/podcast/the-carey-nieuwhof-leadership-podcast/id912753163?i=1000557985976.

5. Tim Keller, "CNLP 339: Tim Keller on How to Bring the Gospel to Post-Christian America, How He'd Preach Today If He was Starting Over Again, Why Founders Get Addicted to Their Churches and Why He Left Redeemer,"

Carey Nieuwhof Leadership Podcast Episode 339, May 2020, https://podcasts.apple.com/gb/podcast/the-carey-nieuwhof-leadership-podcast/id912753163.

6. Kara Powell and Brad M Griffin, *3 Big Questions That Change Every Teenager: Making the Most of Your Conversations and Connections* (Grand Rapids: Baker Books, 2021).

Chapter 12

1. Jay Pathak, "Evangelism: We Share What We Love," Vineyard USA, YouTube, March 2016, https://www.youtube.com/watch?v=rbA3BXbB3A4.

2. Sam Allberry, "Skeptical But Still Reachable Seminar," *Christianity Today* (April 2022), https://www.christianitytoday.com/partners/he-gets-us/skeptical-but-still-reachable.html.

3. Talking Jesus, *Talking Jesus 2022 Report: What People in the UK Think of Jesus, Christians and Evangelism* (April 2022), https://talkingjesus.org/2022-research.

4. Lee Strobel, *The Case for Christ: A Journalist's Personal Investigation of the Evidence for Jesus* (Grand Rapids: Zondervan, 1998).

Chapter 13

1. Malcolm B. Yarnell, "How Art Can Become a Bridge to the Gospel," *International Mission Board* (January 21, 2019), https://www.imb.org/2019/01/21/art-bridge-gospel/.

2. Glenn Phillips and Thomas Crow, eds., *Seeing Rothko* (Los Angeles: Getty Research Institute, 2005), 1.

3. Len Wilson, "5 Ways Creativity is Essential to Your Christian Discipleship," *Len Wilson* (blog), August 2015, https://lenwilson.us/creativity-discipleship/.

4. Donald Miller, "How to Make an Instant Emotional Connection with Your Prospects," *Building a Storybrand*, (2023), https://buildingastorybrand.com/emotional-connection-with-prospects/.

Chapter 14

1. Paul Chappell, "Three Benefits of Practicing Hospitality," *Paul Chappell* (November 2021), https://paulchappell.com/2021/11/01/three-benefits-of-practicing-hospitality/.

2. Dave and Jon Ferguson, *BLESS: 5 Everyday Ways to Love Your Neighbor and Change the World* (Washington, DC: Salem Books, 2021).

3. George G. Hunter III, *The Celtic Way of Evangelism: How Christianity Can Reach the West . . . Again,* Tenth Anniversary Ed. (Nashville: Abingdon Press, 2011).

4. St. Paul's Anglican Church, "Aidan of Lindisfarne," *St. Paul's Anglican Church* (August 2022), https://www.stpaulbarbados.org/aidan-of-lindisfarne/.

Chapter 15

1. Frank Viola and George Barna, *Pagan Christianity?: Exploring the Roots of Our Church Practices* (Carol Stream, IL: Tyndale Momentum, 2008), 99.

2. Louie Giglio, "Indescribable Tour," *Louie Giglio Ministries* (2005), https://www.youtube.com/watch?v=Qh4HcVY2_KE.

Chapter 16

1. American Bible Society, *State of the Bible USA 2022: Research from American Bible Society* (2022), https://sotb.research.bible/.

Chapter 17

1. The All Initiative, "Telling Everyone," *Call2all,* https://www.call2all.org/finish-lines/proclamation-everyone/.

2. Mark Greenwood, "Celebrate every little victory when sharing your faith," *Elim Reach,* https://www.elim.org.uk/Articles/519372/Celebrate_every_little.aspx.

3. Mark Greenwood, *Big Yes Little Yes Healthy Maybe: A New Framework for Evangelism* (Goring by the Sea, UK: Verité CM, 2019).

4. Jim Petersen, *Living Proof: Sharing the Gospel Naturally* (Colorado Springs: NavPress, 1989), 184.